Right Brain WRITING

RIGHT BRAIN WRITING

Right Brain WRITING

CREATIVE SHORTCUTS FOR WORDSMITHS

GARY FEARON

Copyright © 2022 Gary Fearon

All rights reserved. No part of this book may be reproduced without the express written consent of the publisher and the author except in the case of brief quotations in conjunction with articles and reviews.

ISBN: 978-1-7348555-4-8

For everyone who has something good to say

CONTENTS

Section I
BRAINSTORMING
  The Calm Before the Storm 5
  The Big Idea 23
  Lessons in Unexpected Places 43
  Getting Wordy 61

Section II
COMPELLING STORYTELLING
  The Sequence of Events 71
  Pacing 89

Section III
THE CAST OF CHARACTERS
  The Hero 103
  The Adversary 117
  Allies 123

Section IV
KEEPING IT REAL
  Dialogue 145
  Description 153

Section V
BRANDING AND PROMOTION
  The Title 165
  The Cover 171
  Self-Promotion 177

Section VI
THE WRITING LIFE
  Practical Considerations 195
  Accentuate the Positive 207
  Do It Now 219

ACKNOWLEDGMENTS

Words cannot contain my appreciation for the hundreds of writers, authors, poets, playwrights and lyricists I've had the pleasure of brainstorming with, collaborating with, and learning the craft of writing from throughout the years. Their wisdom and friendship are unparalleled sources of inspiration.

Much belated gratitude goes to Steve Allen. The famed TV host, comedian, actor, songwriter, radio DJ, scholar and author graciously took time to encourage my writing when I was yet a teenager. His jack-of-all-trades versatility also taught me that you're allowed to wear many hats and to honor each of them.

Very special thanks to my brother Ron Fearon, a brilliant writer, editor and musician who was among the first to foster my creative side. While I was young, he tutored me in such things as how to play bass, draw a clown, and memorize names. I'm still sorry for punching him in the arm when I was eight.

A BRIEF BUT MEANINGFUL INTRODUCTION

If I were to mention the name J.D. Salinger, most people would think of *Catcher in the Rye*, his first and best-known novel. There is, however, something else Jerome David deserves recognition for. He gave us one of the great quotes about writing:

"Novels grow in the dark."

That was his way of saying that our creative mind continues to work for us even after we turn out the lights. Pulitzer Prize winner Annie Dillard likewise speaks of "imagination" seeing in the dark. Ernest Hemingway was an advocate of turning off his creative mind when he was done writing for the day, knowing that the empty space would renew itself for the next morning's session.

Our subconscious is always processing whatever thoughts we put before it. When we invite our mind to be receptive to an idea, it accepts the call and starts working on our behalf. How often have you wracked your brain trying to remember something, only to let it go, and within a few minutes the answer miraculously appears?

I've lost count of the times a brainstorm has come to me at a time when writing was the last thing on my mind. An almost hypnotic activity like mowing the grass or resting your eyes can trigger a revelation about an existing project or spark a brand new one. Even while we're dreaming, our brain is literally putting thoughts in our head. We may succumb to slumber, but our synapses never nap.

One huge plus to this fountain of creativity is that although our conscious mind tends to be a critic, our subconscious is free from bias. Letting go of the inner editor is where magic happens. We often do our best thinking when we're not trying to think at all.

Which is not to minimize the merit of lucid thought. But our analytical left brain wants to assess things according to whatever set of rules it's accustomed to in any given situation. Allowing ourselves to let our creative right brain take over and think outside the box invites uncharted paths to discovery.

And that's what this book is about. Together we'll explore ways to waken our imagination from its vacation. Like J.D. suggests, we needn't be afraid of the dark. Sometimes that's the best place to detect a glimmer.

SECTION I

BRAINSTORMING

Chapter 1
THE CALM BEFORE THE STORM

"I think 99 times and I find nothing. I stop thinking, swim in silence...and the truth comes to me."

Albert Einstein

Can anyone ignore an approaching storm? A booming thunderbolt and a sudden flash of lightning have no trouble getting our attention. We may sometimes dismiss inclement weather alerts as the rantings of zealous meteorologists, but when a hurricane or a tornado is clearly visible on the horizon, sane people typically seek shelter.

But then there are those who'll intentionally hop in a truck and head right toward the eye of the storm. We may regard them as crazy thrill seekers, yet if you ask these storm chasers why they throw caution to the wind, they actually have some reasonable explanations.

As one might guess, an element of excitement does play a role in their apparent recklessness, but the urge to get up close and personal with severe weather systems is often in the name of science. Professional trackers study the phenomenon in order to learn how to predict their occurrences.

You will find other storm chasers who cite such motivations as curiosity and mystery. Something as unpredictable as Mother Nature offers inherent intrigue. A dedicated tracker may wait for hours in an area where conditions are merely favorable for a storm, hoping for its arrival.

Our brainstorms are just as unpredictable. They are cloaked in mystery as we anticipate when the next one will show up. But you and I both know the exhilaration that comes when a brilliant idea does strike. We're willing to drop everything and focus on it obsessively. By promoting the conditions that make brainstorms possible, we can encourage and even precipitate their arrival.

Throughout *Right Brain Writing*, we'll focus on fun and inventive methods to trigger creative thinking via idea starters and alternate patterns of thinking that you can put to use right away. These concepts have been game changers for me as well as the numerous authors whose brains I've been privileged to pick.

And because the "left brain" skills of communication and language are also essential for writers, we won't ignore *that* hemisphere. What we will do is encourage the two to work together, so that logical left-brainers can also share in the thrill of the hunt.

We can indeed become artful chasers of our own brainstorms. In doing so, we stand to receive the same rewards as these tornado trackers (without the dangers of getting stuck in a flood zone or a cow falling on your truck).

CREATIVE THINKING

"Where do you get your ideas?" is a question most authors have been asked to the point of giving up trying to provide the truest answer. Glib responses such as "I buy them," "I steal them," and "The Tooth Fairy leaves them under my pillow" reflect the fact that ideas come in so many different ways that there is no one-size-fits-all strategy. A story idea may come from a newspaper headline while another may come from an offhand comment overheard at a Wendy's.

Neil Gaiman, author of *Coraline*, did an entire essay on the subject. He said, "You get ideas from daydreaming. You get ideas from being bored. You get ideas all the time. The only difference between writers and other people is we notice when we're doing it."

Gaiman recommends imagining "unconnected and strange things" to make them more memorable. "Often ideas come from two things coming together that haven't come together before."

Fantasy author Mercedes Lackey concurs. "Once you are in the habit of getting ideas," she says, "they come to you without thinking about them. They come from anywhere and anything, but basically they derive from looking at even the most mundane things or circumstances and asking yourself the question, 'What if...'"

Indeed, great stories explore provocative "what if" situations. What if a man invents a time machine? What if a woman learns a family secret? What if aliens invade on a holiday weekend? What if a man were shipwrecked on a desert island for 27 years? What if teenagers had to choose their life's path from one of five factions?

Any story you write will lend itself to a "what if" question. The more intriguing it is, the more curiosity it will provoke.

The creative process, says memoirist Christine Hyung Oak Lee, "is about showing up on the steps each day to greet the Muse, should she choose to stop by. You sweep the steps, waiting . . . Oftentimes the Muse makes no appearance. But if you are not on the steps and the Muse *does* come by, then you miss her. So you wait. You sweep."

Jacqueline Woodson is known to be an idea juggler: "I'm usually working on more than one book at a time. When the ideas stop coming for one, I move on to another one."

Stephen Graham Jones offers this motivating thought: "There are stories out there. There are stories in here. And I'm going as fast as I can, trying to trap them on a page in a way that they can still be alive."

Courtney Milan comes up with multiple ideas and then puts

them together. "I get lots of ideas all the time, and I can't shut them up. But one idea is not a book . . . Eventually, my ideas collide into each other, and once I have enough ideas sticking together, it feels like a book."

Of course, your own experiences are free and ready material for adapting into a story that no one else could write. Taking a slice of your own life, changing the personal details, and adding a "what if" twist is a valid recipe well worth trying.

THE TRUTH ABOUT FICTION

Each of us has an innate sense of curiosity that draws us into questions we'd like to know the answer to. A good "what if" premise is all it takes to make us want to read that book, see that movie, watch that show. We feel as if we won't fully rest until we know the outcome.

Writers from Byron to Mark Twain have been credited with "truth is stranger than fiction" quotes, and indeed, the mysteries of life can be among the most confounding. And when it comes to fiction, few things are more compelling than a situation unlike anything we've ever experienced.

That said, in order for fiction to be credible, it must have truth behind it. Even the most fantastic of plots demands some correspondence with the realities of life as we know it.

If, for example, the premise is "What if a magic device could stop time?", the writer would be wise to examine the ramifications of that question based on the real world. Physics aside, such a premise begs addressing practical considerations like how widespread the effect of the pause is, whether people will still age while in suspended animation, whether air would continue to circulate, etc.

A discerning reader may wonder about such things and appreciate some acknowledgment of them. Even if these explorations don't end up in the book, the writer would do well to feel settled into some personal conclusions about it all.

We may not be experts on a magical device or the world of

the future, but we are experts on reality since we have lived it every day of our lives. That is sufficient fodder for creative storytelling that contains the needed elements of truth.

Whether it's an escape from real life or an exploration of life's possibilities, well-told fiction will always pull us in when it feels real. As *Game of Thrones* writer David Benioff said, "Truth may be stranger than fiction, but it needs a better editor."

EXPLORING THE GREAT UNKNOWN

Tapping into deep creativity often requires letting go of what we know. That is, putting aside our existing expectations and assumptions so we can think outside the box.

For example, let's take the simple act of hanging a picture on the wall. To drive the nail in, our previous experience has taught us to look for a hammer. But in a pinch, a heavy wrench is capable of doing the job. Or maybe we'd rather not put a hole in the wall. We might consider the alternative method of employing one of those non-destructive adhesive strip hangers.

The first solution we are accustomed to isn't necessarily the only one. Sometimes it's not even the best one.

Once upon a time at the grocery store, it would require a cashier to add up your purchases and take your money. Now, UPC codes and digital devices give you the option of checking yourself out and paying with plastic. Things were done the first way for thousands of years, until someone considered that there might be other ways of doing it.

Creative writers are not limited by what they already know or have been told. They are able to generate new ideas, perspectives, and possibilities for any given situation. And that inventiveness can run with carefree abandon by exploring a good "What if."

We're all born with an inherent capability for creativity, but it is something we must practice for it to become second nature. Ultimately, it's limited only by our imagination and the passion to develop it.

TAKE THE LONG WAY HOME

I once had a boss who was fond of having staff meetings, whether we needed them or not. (In his defense, we usually needed them.) During these meetings, Jim would often inject a personal philosophy or something else that was unrelated to work. Perhaps because it wasn't always obvious why he was taking up time with something off topic, most of his wisdom went in one ear and out the other.

But not this pearl, which immediately got our attention: "Tonight, when you leave here, take the long way home." None of us had a clue what this had to do with anything.

"In fact," he added, "get lost."

The staffers looked at each other, wondering if this was his subtle way of telling us we were all fired, or if he simply had lost his mind and we were witnesses to the breakdown we had secretly anticipated for some time. But Jim went on to explain.

"While coming into work today I took a wrong turn and drove through a part of town I hadn't been before. On my way here I saw a house painted pink, unusual businesses I didn't know we had, and a couple of kids drawing chalk pictures on the sidewalk."

Taking all of this in, we were at least semi-assured we weren't fired, and I'm happy to report that his reasoning in thinking we'd benefit from his seemingly random suggestion was actually a rather creative one.

Jim continued by saying that he found himself thinking of pink houses and the type of person who would live in such a house. He considered whether they might be artists, and whether the kids on the sidewalk would grow up to be artists too. He thought about a frame shop he saw right next to a Chinese grocery and pondered what kind of framing is suitable for Chinese rice paper artwork.

His ultimate point was that he dwelt on things he normally wouldn't have thought about, and on this particular day, it opened his mind creatively.

In all honesty, we still didn't quite get it, and those of us who preferred going straight home at night rather than spending time expanding our young minds never altered our route, at least not on purpose. Years later, however, the truth behind our boss's suggestion has rung true for me many times.

Trying out a new restaurant has led to enlightening conversations with owners about why we like the flavors we like. Visiting a sick friend at the hospital elicits strong reactions in the presence of countless details we don't think about in daily life. Even sitting for a moment at the mall to take in the hubbub can inspire elaborate imaginary stories about total strangers.

The muse is constantly feeding us ideas and information we can make use of in our writing, but we're often too ingrained in our usual path and our typical way of thinking to notice them. Looking back, haven't some of your most original ideas come out of the blue when you've been out of your familiar territory?

You may be wondering, as we did, why our boss suggested we take an alternate route home that night, instead of following his example the next morning and coming into the office all inspired.

He didn't want us to be late for work.

GET LOST ... IN YOUR WRITING

During the years I spent as Creative Director for *Southern Writers Magazine*, I had the privilege of picking the brains of countless bestselling wordsmiths. For one particular article, I asked a group of selected authors this question:

"Who do you trust to read your first draft?"

Karen White, Marji Laine, Hope Denney, Joy Ross Davis, Randy Ingermanson, Cindy Woodsmall, Stephanie Bennett, E.E. Kennedy, Bryan E. Powell, and Connie Chastain gave answers that turned out to be as diverse as the genres they write in. The lucky readers of their first raw drafts ran the gamut from fellow writers and editors to trusted relatives and close friends.

It takes some fortitude to fork over your hard-fought words for their first reading. To do this with confidence, the authors choose their first readers with care. By making a discriminating selection, they are assured of getting constructive feedback which will be valuable for their first rewrite.

Getting to the end of a first draft is usually a mix of relief and anxiety, excitement and dread. But because your book has made it to the finish line, hopefully any rewrites can be met with empowerment.

Unfortunately, most writers never make it to that point. The reasons can be many, but far too often they lose their initial spark via too much self-editing, diluting their creativity. Even the most experienced authors can become their own worst enemy midway through the first draft by listening to the negative voice of self-judgment.

That's when many authors find it helpful to try to separate themselves from their writing. An intuitive method is to think of ourselves as a conduit, rather than a creator. Steven Pressfield, the author of *The War of Art: Break Through the Blocks & Win Your Inner Creative Battles*, is a proponent of learning to let go and listen to inspiration. He writes:

"This is [a] secret that real artists know and wannabe writers don't. When we sit down each day and do our work, power concentrates around us. The Muse takes note of our dedication. She approves. We have earned favor in her sight. When we sit down and work, we become like a magnetized rod that attracts iron filings. Ideas come. Insights form."

Zen masters go on long journeys to find themselves. More accurately, to lose themselves. Achieving the elevated state some call "no mind" may not sound easy to do when you're living with yourself 24/7, but in the creative arts it's well worth the effort to exert *no* effort.

By abandoning the critical you, you make room for the inspiration and resulting motivation that's clamoring to get back in.

When your creativity gets stuck, step outside yourself and stop, look and listen for what's just beyond you. If you're lucky you'll get completely lost, and your story will bring you home.

EVERYONE'S A CRITIC

The hardest part of letting go can be learning to quiet that inner critic. Too often, we readily dismiss an idea worth exploring, either because it takes us out of familiar territory or because we think others may not "get" it.

One of my most important life lessons came in grade school. The teacher gave us each a piece of manila paper and told us to draw and color a picture of a house with a tree in the yard. (Even at that young age, most of us recognized that our creativity was already stifled by being given paper that was tan in color. But that wasn't the lesson.)

Dutifully I drew my masterpiece, taking special care to get the angles and dimensions as accurate as any 10-year-old could, and when it came time to color it, I got out my diverse spectrum of eight crayons and diligently made the tree leaves many shades of green through varying strengths of blue and yellow. As I handed in my finished product, I wondered whether the teacher would be more impressed with my sophisticated shading technique or the fact that I'd made a perfect frame-within-a-frame, coloring just up to a half an inch around all borders, rather like an old photograph.

"Why didn't you color to the edges?" she denounced.

Taken aback by her displeasure, but just as quickly reinforced by the artistic ground I had to stand on, I said, "I made a frame for it."

"It doesn't need a frame! The paper is the frame! You should have colored to the edges!"

Well, she never told us that. Nor did she tell us what many of us eventually had to learn on our own, which is: Not everyone appreciates artistic expression, and if you're not careful there will be plenty who shoot you down when you don't do things the way they would do it.

In retrospect, I recall that this teacher normally taught math and science, two subjects based in facts which don't waver from their cut-and-dried course. I can now understand why letting my Crayolas go on a wild journey signaled anarchy. I can only hope the school of life has since been equally educational for her and that she has come to realize that in the creative arts, 1 plus 1 doesn't always equal 2.

It's sad to consider all the art classes—and writing classes—out there and wonder how many students have not gone on to become artists or writers because someone in authority told them they 'couldn't' do something or did it wrong, only to lose confidence in their muse.

The trick is being able to distinguish constructive criticism from destructive disapproval that has roots in ignorance or even jealousy. Like Karen White and the other authors previously mentioned, you can't go wrong surrounding yourself with critics of quality…peers and mentors who have your best interest at heart. As your own worst critic, you deserve to give yourself even more latitude.

It took a while, plus the advice of much more sophisticated art teachers and writing friends, for me to rediscover not only the pleasure of creative expression but the truth behind it, which is that real art is allowed to break the rules when it has a reason to.

In the words of Mark Twain: "Get your facts first, and then you can distort them as you please."

Happy distorting!

THE DREAM TEAM

What did you dream last night? If you're like most people, you either can't remember any or don't think you dreamed at all. Fact is, according to researchers, each of us dream every night, but the majority of those dreams leave our memory when we wake up.

Why some of them stick and others don't, I leave up to the experts in physiology and psychology to explain. I just know it has something to do with how much Taco Bell I had.

Particularly worth trying to remember are recurring dreams, which are said to keep presenting themselves to teach us something or help us resolve some issue. My most recurring dream takes me back to junior high school, where I am looking for my next class but must wander the halls because I can't find my class schedule. If, by chance, you have that same dream, please tell me where my locker is.

Most of us tend to write off dreams as the figments of our imagination that they are, paying little heed to them. But have you ever thought about taking a dream and turning it into a story?

These famous writers did just that.

Stephenie Meyer had no aspirations of becoming a writer until she had a vivid dream about the star-crossed lovers who became the protagonists of *Twilight*. She merely wanted to capture the story for herself so she wouldn't forget these characters who fascinated her.

Stephen King was napping on a flight to London when he dreamed of a woman holding a writer prisoner and torturing him. Excited by this premise, the first thing King did upon arrival was write the first 40 or 50 pages of what became *Misery*.

In 1885, the wife of Robert Louis Stevenson woke him from a nightmare when he complained, "Why did you wake me? I was dreaming a fine bogey tale." Indeed, he was in the middle of a dream about a man transforming into a murderer, and *The Strange Case of Dr Jekyll and Mr Hyde* soon hit the streets.

And then there's the granddaddy of all spook stories, *Frankenstein*. Mary Shelley had been in the company of scientists and speculators whose conversation included the occult. Her resulting nightmare involved a mad scientist trying to play God by creating a man.

Before you conclude that dreams have only been used to advantage by writers of the paranormal, other books as diverse as *Stuart Little* and *Sophie's Choice* are said to have their origins in dreams. I know for a fact that's true of *Stuart Little*, but I can't substantiate *Sophie's Choice*. Maybe I dreamed it.

The point is, the premise of your next dream could just possibly become the plot for a great novel by repurposing it as a story possibility.

Dreaming of writing the next bestseller? Consider teaming up with your nocturnal narratives and perhaps they will do some of the work for you.

PERIODICAL INSPIRATION

You never do know where a good story idea may appear. In physicians' waiting rooms, for example, you'll often see magazines designed to appeal to multiple interests and age groups. While waiting for a dental checkup recently, I observed a particularly wide variety.

Being both a movie and news junkie, I'll often reach first for an *Entertainment Weekly* or a *Newsweek* if they have it. But on this occasion, I decided to broaden my horizons and look at magazines I would never normally read, purely in the interests of inspiration and enlightenment. And perhaps material for this book.

The first magazine I picked up dealt with outdoor adventure, a radical enough choice to start with, since my loyalties firmly lie with the great indoors. Pledging to read whatever article I randomly opened to, I found myself learning about the Beer Mile, a fad from Australia which challenges runners to complete four laps around a quarter-mile track within five minutes, downing a brewski at each lap. Apparently, few participants can handle consuming all that ale, and I must admit that I bailed on the article when I realized that it consumed eight pages of the magazine. But it left me interested in the fact that the organizers of these events almost have to do so under the radar because of health risks and legal ramifications.

Another magazine—one that I really had to bite the bullet to pick up—was a golfing magazine. The first page I came to featured a Q&A with an expert on country clubs across America. A reader asked what course he might recommend for a vacation spot based on his personal preferences of a warm climate, nearness to a historical site, and whatever. Before I put that mag back, I considered the value of planning a trip based on very specific criteria, such as researching a city one might want to set their next novel in.

My third magazine was about living in trailer parks (which made me wonder a little about my dentist). The page I opened to happened to be an advertisement for a racetrack where their spring weekend event would include entertainment provided by Beatles tribute band Ticket to Ride. The next night was to be headlined by a Neil Diamond tribute band. I had no idea there was such a thing as a Neil Diamond tribute *band*, and it made me wonder what other tribute bands might exist that I don't know about.

Soon after that, I was summoned for my appointment, but not before I took stock of the new insights I had gleaned from this free source of inspiration. In that short span of time, I was given the nucleus of a story idea involving a fan so infatuated with their favorite singer that they move to his city and organize a questionable event they know the singer will want to be a part of, and mayhem ensues. In fact, if you'd like to write it, go for it because I'll be busy working on my tribute band. I do a passable Louis Prima.

All of this is a way of saying that I recommend branching out and reading something off the beaten path. You might find similar pages of rewarding randomness while standing in a checkout line, but the opportunity to take your time and expand your mind in the relative comfort and quietude of a waiting room could be just what the doctor ordered.

SPINNING THE CREATIVE WHEEL

One of the greatest inventions of the 20th century—or any

century, in my opinion—was a piece of cardboard with a spinner dial and a bunch of words printed on it called The Laugh Finder. If you're a creative person I think you'll share my awe once I tell you of its magic powers.

In younger years, my numerous pursuits included that of a correspondence course in cartooning. When the big box of introductory materials arrived, it contained many books of lessons, an assortment of artist pencils, a posable wooden marionette, and the aforementioned curiosity.

The idea behind The Laugh Finder is that it would help you create the idea for a cartoon. You'd spin it several times, and via an enormous list that corresponded to the numbers on the dial, you'd get your characters, props and the "basis of humor" (aka the situation). Instant hilarity, right?

A typical session with The Laugh Finder might yield you these results:

"Mummy" ... "Hearing aid" ... "Weakness".

What humorous cartoon could you come up with involving a mummy, a hearing aid and weakness?

After some thought you might concoct something like this. We see Dracula talking to an elderly mummy who's using an ear horn to hear. Dracula says, "You think you've got problems? How'd you like to have tired blood and it's not even yours?"

Let's go for another spin. "Old man" ... "Waitress" ... "Doing things the hard way".

How about this? An old couple is sitting at a restaurant table. The wife is chowing down while the man hasn't touched his meal. The waitress asks if his food is okay. Through a puckered mouth, he tells the waitress, "Yes, everything's fine. I'm just waiting for Maw to finish using the teeth."

Groans aside (and I'm right there with you), perhaps you can see the value of this concept. The principle of taking disparate things and combining them in a new framework (for humor or other purposes) has been a valuable tool that I continue to find useful almost every day.

Don't know where to go with a character in your story? You could spin in a new twist by picking a couple of words at random from a magazine or the dictionary. "Inadequate" and "clean" are two I just found. Maybe your protagonist isn't a great housekeeper, a trait that can lend itself to some interesting and very human development in your tale. Perhaps an earring they step on leads to a minor emergency room visit where they meet the doctor of their dreams. Or a vampire with anemia.

When we feel a little stuck creatively, we may not have the ingenious Laugh Finder handy to point us in a new direction, but if we think outside the box it's easy to come up with something unexpected we could add to the mix. That could be all it takes to put a new spin on things.

THE NEXT BIG THING

Last December, as I approached my living room to eat lunch, I heard a woman singing "O Come All Ye Faithful" on the TV. *There must be a Christmas concert on*, I figured. When I arrived, it turned out to be Carol Brady singing in her church, circa 1969.

It was the Brady Bunch's first Christmas as a blended family. All the kids were there, smiling proudly from the pews as their mother sang *Oh come, let us adore him, Christ our Lord*. Little Cindy gave her new stepdad a grateful smile when he put his arm around her. Their maid Alice might have even been present, comically tearing up as she often did during any tender moment.

While I watched, I could only think how unlikely it would be for such a scene to appear on a modern-day sitcom. Even on TV Land, where this vintage show was airing, the newer comedies feature anything but a wholesome family unit. If alien lifeforms tuned into today's TV they would assume that everyone on Earth is divorced and cranky.

Entertainment gets less innocent and more cynical as each

year passes. We see it in books, films, music, art, everywhere we look. In a world where Hannah Montanas become Miley Cyruses, it's a fair question to ask, "What's happening?"

Part of the answer is, we are wired to always be looking for the next big thing. And, by its nature, the next big thing can't be like the old thing. There has to be something extra, and the trend has always been to make it more extreme.

Take young adult fiction. It wasn't that long ago when Harry Potter stirred up a cauldron of controversy. A short time later, the tide turned toward vampires. Riding the bloody waves of *Twilight*, there have been books and movies such as *Abraham Lincoln, Vampire Hunter*. I expect any day now to see *Benjamin Franklin, Zombie Slayer*.

The Hardy Boys have given way to *The Hunger Games*. Nancy Drew is now *Divergent*. Bold and imaginative, these new series are replacing G-rated treasure map mysteries with dark, dystopian survival epics. Critics fear they encourage rebellion while fans praise them for the theme of overcoming suppression. Either way, they sell like hotcakes.

On TV and in movies, portrayals of sex, drugs and violence are off the charts, alongside language that used to be considered not ready for prime time. Edgy sells. Controversy gets headlines.

Without even debating the rightness or wrongness of any of the above, one does have to wonder where it will end. How much further can we go before all sense and sensibility, values and virtues live only in nostalgia?

I applaud the many writers I have known who strive for something better. These are the ones who realize it's possible to grab a reader's attention without offending half their audience. They weave a masterful tale and leave the reader feeling like they've traveled a high road and not spent the weekend in Gomorrah.

As we brainstorm together in this book, I invite you to buck what some call progress and follow the road less traveled. If more authors and audiences demanded it, maybe the next big thing could be a return to something that's easy to feel is gone forever.

Together we could make Alice cry more happy tears.

RIGHT BRAIN WRITING

Chapter 2
THE BIG IDEA

"Don't worry about people stealing your ideas. If your ideas are any good, you'll have to ram them down some people's throats."

Howard Aiken

ALWAYS ON THE LOOKOUT

When an idea comes to us, we make a judgment call of its value almost immediately. We ask ourselves: Is it worth doing? Is it possible to do? Do I even want to do it?

The decision of whether or not a given idea deserves to be given a chance is often left up to our gut feeling, and rightly so, since intuition can be more instinctual than judgmental evaluation. If we allow our inner critic to make the call, we may conclude that it's not original enough, we don't have the time to do it, or someone else could do it better. A lot of good ideas are left on the table and forgotten.

Fortunately, in some of those magic moments of inspiration, we do recognize ideas that are worth holding on to, and—much like the proverbial light bulb over the head—we feel instantly illumined. These ideas fill us with such enthusiasm that we can think of nothing else. They nag us until we do something about them.

Some of these ideas, we will indeed see through to completion. Others we'll jump into with enthusiasm only to lose momentum after a few chapters—or, worse, a few paragraphs—and they end up on the cutting room floor with the rest of our creative castaways.

A good barometer for evaluating an idea is to ask yourself, *Does this idea excite me? Does it inspire me?* If you find that you're already heady with enthusiasm, you're well on the way to seeing your brainchild come to life. Because what makes the difference is how much *passion* we bring to the project.

We normally think of passion as an earnest pursuit of something. But dictionaries include its additional meaning, one that relates to sacrifice and suffering (as in *The Passion of the Christ*). If we really believe in something, we're willing to put in the effort. When it matters enough to us, we make it happen.

Sue Grafton said, "Ideas are easy. It's the *execution* of ideas that really separates the sheep from the goats." I'm not sure how many of us have aspired to goathood, but we sure want to get that Great American Novel written.

So how do we find that good idea in the first place? We know from the great writers—and from our own experience—that the best way to land a good idea is to come up with a lot of them. We can do that by training ourselves to be on the lookout for them everywhere we go.

An interesting conversation I had with a fellow who has been a postal carrier for thirty years sticks with me. At one point in my childhood I wanted to be a mailman, so I had a fair share of questions that he seemed to enjoy answering. But the most memorable thing he had to say wasn't related to delivering packages or avoiding getting bit by dogs.

Years ago, when his daughter was very young, he would bring her to the post office on Take Your Daughter to Work Day. She helped him sort the mail for his route in the appropriate slots, and on one occasion she drew him a picture, which he proudly hung in his cubicle. That drawing has hung in the same place for years.

His daughter is in her late twenties now, so that picture holds precious memories for him. As you can imagine, he wasn't happy when a supervisor told him he had to take it down. "No personal items in the workspace," they said. He knew the fact that it had already hung there for two decades would not be enough of a defense. So he replied, "Then that coffee cup on your desk and those pictures of your family need to go too." That ended the conversation, and the drawing still hangs.

As he related this to me, I considered the fact that this little episode from his life told me a great deal about the stranger I had just met. In a short time, I discovered that 1) he is a family man, 2) he is sentimental, and 3) he can stand up for himself. If these were traits you wanted to convey in your novel's protagonist, a scenario such as this would be far more memorable than simply describing him as a sentimental family man. We bond with a character when we observe our own humanity in him/her.

By itself, incidents like this aren't story ideas as much as they are anecdotes. But stories come in all forms and fashions, and what seems like a simple premise could easily be built upon and turned into a major storyline or at least a noteworthy plot point. A man getting shorted on his change at the sub shop is barely an anecdote. But if it's the last straw in his already unstable life, it could be the basis for a crime novel.

A classic newspaper credo states that even the most boring report can become fascinating with the right sidenote or quote included. A good journalist looks for that unique angle to give the story its punch. Sometimes interviewing the quietest witness yields the biggest revelation.

Author and freelance writer Brad Herzog says he finds those captivating twists by looking at the "fine print." Digging into the little details that are often overlooked help the former newspaper reporter discover the most intriguing aspect of a story to pursue.

Like most people, author Peter Benchley assumed it was safe to swim at the beach until he came across a newspaper article about a shark that was terrorizing an East Coast community. This new consideration led to *Jaws*, riding the relatively new wave known as the disaster movie.

Whether we hear about them from someone else, or live them in our own lives, every day we are witness to countless moments that could be the starting point for the next story or scene we write. If we are keen observers as well as creative writers, we'll never run out of ideas.

SEE IT IN A DIFFERENT LIGHT

"A change is as good as a rest," my grandmother used to say. I thought she came up with that one herself until I grew up and heard that other people's grandparents said the same thing. It took me almost that long to appreciate the truth of that proverb.

A musician friend of mine jokes that when he starts to feel songwriter's block, it's time to buy a new instrument. (This fellow, for the record, has more guitars than songs he's actually written.) There is, however, validity to that concept. If you're a musician who plays keyboard, noodling around on a new synthesizer and having a different variety of sounds at your fingertips will get fresh ideas rolling around. It inspires chords and progressions you never thought to try before.

Professional photographers know that the difference between a good photo and a great photo is often in the lighting. You can be as keen and adventurous as you please with the camera angle, aperture settings and much more, but in the end, the proper illumination is critical to capture a classic shot.

As writers, we seek to capture our vision through the lens of our pens. When we find it hard to see what that vision is, it can help to see it in a different light, by taking in a change of scenery or trying a fresh approach.

If you write at your desk all the time, you're attached to the same keyboard, desk, walls, pictures on those walls, etc. Indeed, there's plenty to be said for familiarity, and the quiet environment of our office can be preferable to a busy coffee shop (unless you're Sandra Balzo and you're crafting Coffeehouse Mysteries).

But sometimes a bustling, noisy environment can be just the ticket to rouse your muse. Has your mind ever taken a road less traveled while sitting on a mall bench, observing the madding crowd and pondering their backstory? When you're away on vacation, aren't you itching to get back to your computer because of all the new ideas you can't wait to write?

If you write nonfiction exclusively, try your hand at a fiction piece; and vice versa. If you write all your stories starting at the beginning, try writing the ending first and see how the story that precedes it virtually writes itself. If you outline your novels, try writing your next one freeform. You're guaranteed to see your familiar craft in a new light.

Creativity finds its nucleus in change. We can emulate something that's gone before, but to make it something of our own requires taking it in a different direction. Often, that begins with us trying something new ourselves. As the saying goes, "If you want something you've never had, then you've got to do something you've never done before."

When she told us that a change is as good as a rest, my grandma merely sought to convey that a change of pace can restore peace within. Change can be the very spark that ignites the creative fire inside of us, which is a writer's continual hope. Thanks, Grammy.

A NEW POINT OF VIEW

From the beginning of tale telling, the classic stories have been rewritten again and again, thanks to new sets of characters in new settings that differentiate things enough to make it all seem brand new again. But another interesting tactic is to tell an established tale from another character's point of view. Perhaps one of your own works will someday be suited to such a reimagining.

I can't say I've read any of the books, but I have it on good authority that the popular *Fifty Shades of Grey* books have a counterpart series, flipping the same story to the guy's point of view. With the release of *Grey*, author E.L. James managed more mileage from her popular trilogy by painting additional shades of grey.

Twilight likewise enjoyed a reincarnation by its original author, Stephenie Meyer. In a reversal of genders, this time the male vampire Edward was a female vampire named Edythe, and Bella was a young male named Beau. I can only guess there was a love triangle involving a wolfgirl.

Veronica Roth gave fans of *Divergent* new insight into its male co-star when she released *Four*, a collection of short stories from character Four's POV. An additional point of interest is that Roth said she had originally written *Divergent* from Four's perspective and that its female heroine came into being only after the first draft.

The latest revival of the Tony Award-winning musical *Company* flips the main character, formerly a confirmed bachelor named Bobby, into a female lead named Bobbie. With playwright Stephen Sondheim's blessing, the director said it gave the show more potency, asserting that a 35-year-old single woman of today feels more urgency to settle down than her male counterpart.

A fair amount of such retreads can be found in fan fiction, though the trend to turn the tables has been going on for some time. *Wicked*, turning the wicked witch of Oz into a sympathetic character, was the frontrunner in only the more recent crop of reimaginings.

Back to the Future dabbled with multiple POVs in its sequels, when we got to see bad guy Biff's reactions and interactions with events we had seen in the first film. Marty himself encountered his own pasts and futures through new eyes as he traveled through time.

From Peter Rabbit to The Three Little Pigs, kiddie tales have long lived happily ever after via rewrites that let the villain tell their side of the story.

But fantasies and fairy tales aren't the only stories able to benefit from a shift in perspective. We can use this method as a way to elaborate on the conflict between two characters with opposing viewpoints. Or a close examination of our story may reveal that the strongest point of view belongs to a character other than the protagonist.

The point of view we choose to convey can liven things up by telling more than one side of the story. As Abraham Lincoln said, "We can complain because rose bushes have thorns, or rejoice because thorn bushes have roses." A difference of opinion makes things interesting, and we can all agree on that.

THE SPICE OF LIFE

A friend of mine shares his childhood memories of the "family movie night" that was a weekly ritual in his home. Each member of the family got to take turns picking the flick of the week at Blockbuster. As you can predict, the kids always picked out movies geared toward talking animals while the adults chose more sophisticated fare.

For every Ninja Turtles movie they watched, my friend's dad had them sit down to a classic like *On the Waterfront* or *A Streetcar Named Desire*. One week it was even *Cat on a Hot Tin Roof*. (Don't worry, grade school exposure to these mature themes didn't scar the young boy for life; in fact, he went on to become a youth pastor).

It harkened me back to thoughts of my youth, which included a lavish movie house with a balcony, lush curtains that opened and closed, and a counter where you could buy expensive souvenir programs for the epics being shown. I think even more than the movies themselves, my parents enjoyed introducing their children to this edifying environment. So I, too, grew up on a well-balanced diet of comedies, dramas, romances, and musicals, as well a couple of movies my parents made us walk out on.

Looking back, I'm deeply grateful for this early education, which gives me a pretty good understanding today of the elements that go into a comedy, a drama, a romance, or a musical, not to mention movies my parents would still walk out on. And no doubt you can say the same.

While we may have a favorite genre of movie—let's say *spy thriller*—that doesn't keep us from attending the occasional romantic comedy that catches our interest.

Which brings me to this question: Do you read more than one genre? Do you always read the same genre, or do you mix it up? Granted, committing to an entire novel requires a greater time investment than a two-hour movie (unless you're one of those superhumans who can read a book a night).

Just as we moviegoers have cut our storytelling teeth by watching a variety of film genres, veering from our usual reading course to pick up an author who writes the kind of tale we're unfamiliar with will introduce us to other ways of telling a story. The intricacies specific to another genre could be eye-opening and even help add a new dimension to the genre we normally write in.

Pulitzer Prize-winning columnist Mary Schmich said, "Good art is art that allows you to enter it from a variety of angles and to emerge with a variety of views." I look forward to adding a little more variety to my library, and I hope new ideas will emerge for you too.

For now, I can't let a mention of Mary Schmich go by without sharing one of her greatest claims to fame, a commencement speech called "Everybody's Free to Wear Sunscreen" which Baz Luhrmann turned into a music video (easily found on YouTube). It's a laundry list of brilliant advice that could change your life. I guarantee it will at least change five minutes of your life.

BRAINSTORM TRIGGERS YOU CAN USE RIGHT NOW

Writing prompts

Anytime you're stuck for an idea and need something to warm up your writing chops with, the Internet can be your best friend. Googling "writing prompts" will yield an endless supply of story starters. These can be especially useful for journaling or memoir writing if something personal like "Write about your favorite Christmas memory" or "What's your biggest pet peeve" gets you inspired.

For fiction writers, there are several websites that will

generate a random first line for your story. Could you do something with one of the following openers? These are samples directly borrowed from the very useful site found at http://writingexercises.co.uk/firstlinegenerator.php

> "He'd had a bad day and just needed something to make him feel better."

> "The horse came back alone."

> "The whole family had been cursed since..."

That same site generates story titles, characters, plots, subplots, names, settings and much more. Once you visit writingexercises.co.uk you may find yourself spending many creative hours exploring inspiration at random.

Finding the muse in music

When talking to writers, I'm always curious to learn whether they like to listen to music while they work, or prefer to have it as quiet as possible. Being aurally oriented myself, I enjoy knowing that many authors choose music that fits the mood of whatever they're writing. Many use free music websites such as AccuRadio to provide a running backdrop of soundtracks ranging from romance to horror. They pick a genre and the playlist comes up automatically.

That atmospheric approach provides effective support when you have decided on your premise. But have you ever considered turning to music as a way of inspiring an idea? Songs are another readily-available source of story starters that are easily overlooked.

Song titles

A good song title can make an ideal writing prompt. Don't each of these classic phrases conjure something you could build a scenario around?

Heartbreak Hotel
Born to Run
Blowin' in the Wind
King of the Road
Behind Closed Doors
When Doves Cry
Don't Stand So Close to Me

If you're worried about stealing an existing song title, don't worry, baby. Songwriters are especially prone to borrow a good idea for themselves. Over the years, each of these titles have been used ten times or more for very different songs:

Call Me
Crazy
Hold On
I Want You
Runaway
Smile
Stay
Without You

Song titles can't be copyrighted any more than novel titles can. Even a more involved title like "Have I Told You Lately That I Love You" has been used more than once, in entirely distinct hits for Gene Autry and Rod Stewart. Steal away.

Story songs

Country music in particular has provided a wealth of songs that tell a story. Premises like these could be given different titles, different characters, and spelled out into entirely new tales:

Ode to Billie Joe
The Night the Lights Went Out in Georgia
Harper Valley P.T.A.
Coward of the County

(For the record, all of the above became critically panned movies or TV shows. I'm sure you can do better.)

Clichés

A well-known phrase has the benefit of familiarity to resonate immediately and sound classic. The writers of these songs can attest to that:

Bad Blood
Bad to the Bone
Every Rose Has Its Thorn
One Bad Apple
Over My Head
Take It Easy
That's What Friends Are For
You Ain't Seen Nothin' Yet

Random sentences from novels

Here are a few phrases I grabbed just now from the middle of three random books in my office.

"It soon became clear, first to his family, then to the village, that he had changed."

"He was overcome with emotion, with dreams of her in their younger days, the youthful beauty that he had taken for granted and had been lucky enough to find again."

"He told his secretary that he was in the States on a special assignment. She was a bit hurt by his secrecy, but thought nothing more of it."

Any of these could be trigger a decent story idea. In fact, writing prompts aren't just useful for creating a new story; they can also come in handy in the middle of a novel when things need to take a dramatic turn.

WHEN GENRES COLLIDE

One can only guess what Jane Austen would think of the novel *Pride and Prejudice and Zombies*. In 2009, author Seth Grahame-Smith and Quirk Books cleverly capitalized on a current hot topic by sinking their teeth into Austen's 1813 classic, creating a new novel of manners and monsters. ("You are as ferocious as you are fetching," declares Mr Darcy.) A movie of the same name made it to theaters in February 2016.

Call it a parody, call it a mashup, but whatever you do, don't call it a one hit wonder. *Pride and Prejudice and Zombies* started a zombie apocalypse of its own, inspiring other authors to write such twisted tomes as:

Alice in Zombieland
Sense and Sensibility and Sea Monsters
Little Women and Werewolves
William Shakespeare's Star Wars: The Empire Striketh Back
Grave Expectations
Android Karenina

Grahame-Smith continued to contribute more of his own fangy fare with 2010's *Abraham Lincoln: Vampire Hunter*.

Even fairy tales have not been safe from those who would rewrite history. *That Risen Snow: A Scary Tale of Snow White and Zombies* picks up where happily ever after leaves off. It turns out that Snow's resurrection doesn't come without a certain complication. Which makes me fear for Sleeping Beauty, who was dead to the world even longer than Snow by the time her prince showed up.

More than simply grabbing the coattails of a passing fancy, a good hybrid novel not only captures the spirit of the original material but adds its own page-turning twists. Another popular genre, Steampunk, shares a similar premise of mixing the ordinary with the extraordinary. In this, H.G. Wells was well before his time.

Author Kerry Nietz once told me how he came up with his

2014 novel *Amish Vampires in Space:* "For me, it was an interesting mental challenge. Could I intersect three genres—Science Fiction, Amish, and Vampires—and produce a compelling and plausible story?" Nietz succeeded, and even followed up with 2015's *Amish Zombies in Space* and 2019's *Amish Werewolves in Space.*

Perhaps you can think of other mashup possibilities. I know I would enjoy a novel in which Sherlock Holmes matches wits with The Mad Hatter. These two insane geniuses on opposite ends of the mental health spectrum would make for a very fun read indeed.

But let's not stop there. Might I also suggest these titles, just ripe for the writing:

Calamity Jane Eyre
Little Orphan Annie of Green Gables
Green Eggs and Hamlet

With so many genre mashups yet to be tapped, don't be dismayed if the zombie and vampire trend isn't the particular bandwagon you feel like hopping on. All you need is a little imagination to cook up another idea worth bringing to life.

FOLLOW THE YELLOW BRICK ROAD

When the Broadway show *Wicked* came to town recently, my oldest friend was dragged kicking and screaming by his wife, who had been waiting years to see it. My friend's reluctance was multifaceted, but the bulk of it had to do with his distaste for musicals. (This is the same guy who'll spend five months out of the year watching *American Idol.*)

Having already experienced this tuneful, colorful modern spectacle myself, I was hoping my friend would emerge from the theater a changed man, on whom *Wicked*—and the Great American Musical in general—would have worked its magic.

"I'd rather go through four root canals than sit through that again," was his next-day review, or something similarly periodontal.

"Didn't you like the songs?" I asked.

"The songs were fine," he replied, as were the performances, the costumes, the sets, and everything else I asked about.

"Then what didn't you like?" I pressed.

"They ruined it."

"What do you mean, they ruined it?"

"They changed the story."

He didn't mean it wasn't *The Wizard of Oz* we all remember; he knew that much going in. What he objected to was that they introduced different backstories and relationships for the main characters, adding new twists to familiar plot points.

"It's ridiculous," he insisted. "It would never happen that way." His indignation was so dramatic that I thought he was joking, but he was as serious as a house falling on you.

Now, I respect the L. Frank Baum classic as much as anyone; in fact, I often refer to it as a prime example of the "Hero's Journey" storytelling roadmap. Yet *Wicked's* reinvention of the original characters didn't disturb me any more than the multitudinous cinematic variations of my childhood idol Batman. Many of us find revisionist interpretations to be creative and unpredictable, leaving us pondering fresh possibilities. And of course, it's merely a reimagining which doesn't have to replace the beloved classic.

But here's the deal. *The Wizard of Oz* has been revisited hundreds—if not thousands—of times, using entirely different characters and settings. In how many books and screenplays has the protagonist been sent to a strange world, met new allies and mentors along the way and had to conquer their greatest enemy before they could reach their goal? Sometimes a scarecrow, a tin man and a cowardly lion are portrayed as a gunslinger, a robot and a Chewbacca. May the force be with you, Dorothy.

Novelist Gail Godwin had a good explanation for why we don't rebel against retreads. To paraphrase: There are only a few stories worth telling, which is why they need to be told over and over again, until everyone recognizes them as their own experience.

Virtually every tale we tell as writers—whether intentionally or inadvertently—will have some correlation to the great classics. Part of the fun is discovering the new spin we can put on the same old story.

Personally, I like knowing why the Wicked Witch was green.

NOTHING NEW UNDER THE SUN

Adapting an existing story is nothing new. It's been done for centuries. This is because there is a need to tell these stories in a different way, with fresh ideas, or to reach a wider audience.

There are countless examples of adaptations that have been successful and that have gone on to become classics themselves—such as the Disney adaptations of *Snow White* and *Cinderella*, and more recently, *Rapunzel (Tangled)* and *The Princess and the Frog*. Disney built a better mousetrap by taking the grim out of these Grimm's fairy tales.

Fans of *West Side Story* are well aware that it's a modern-day variation of *Romeo & Juliet*. Less known is that Shakespeare adapted his classic tragedy from a 1562 poem by Arthur Brooke, "The Tragicall Historye (sic) of Romeus and Juliet". *That* poem was based on an Italian novella by Matteo Bandello. And if we fully trace the story's DNA, we can go all the way back to Ovid's *Metamorphoses* in 8 A.D. to see that this thing had legs.

When Solomon wrote that there is "nothing new under the sun," he emphasized the consistency of creation—how the sun is always in the sky and how mankind has a habit of repeating itself. What we experience, however innovative it may seem, is simply a variation on an existing theme.

Putting a new spin on a classic story doesn't translate to a lack of creativity. It's an opportunity for the writer to explore how you would perceive the same story and how it can be told differently in another time period or culture.

LIKE ROBINSON CRUSOE

Gilligan and his fellow island castaways would have appreciated the empathetic title Daniel Defoe gave his most famous work. The first edition of his classic tale was titled *The Life and Strange Surprizing (sic) Adventures of Robinson Crusoe, of York, Mariner: Who lived Eight and Twenty Years, all alone in an uninhabited Island on the Coast of America, near the Mouth of the Great River of Oroonoque; Having been cast on Shore by Shipwreck, wherein all the Men perished but himself. With an Account how he was at last as strangely deliver'd by Pirates.*

The title alone is a three-hour tour.

When we think of the story of Robinson Crusoe, the only thing most of us recall is a man stranded on an island. If we remember anything else, it might be his companion Friday. There is actually a lot more to the story before and after his years as a castaway, but if we ever knew it, it pales in our memory next to the main crisis. His particular predicament is one that's popularly revisited in both drama and comedy. For example:

My Favorite Wife (1940, comedy) Irene Dunne has seven years of bad luck marooned on a desert island.

Swiss Family Robinson (1960, adventure) An entire family is shipwrecked.

Blue Lagoon (1980, romance) Brooke Shields finds jungle love with a fellow castaway.

Cast Away (2000, drama) Tom Hanks has meaningful dialogues with a volleyball while stranded in the South Pacific.

Nomadland (2020, drama) A woman living in her van learns the ways of other homeless sojourners.

Hmm, did you notice the years of release? Following this twenty-year pattern, we can expect another one in 2040. There's your cue to start writing it, somebody.

Other variations on the "You can't go home again" theme have visited a variety of locales:

Lost in Space (TV series, 1965-68, sci-fi) Swiss Family Robinson in the cosmos.

Planes, Trains and Automobiles (1987, comedy) John Candy and Steve Martin encounter one impediment after another while trying to get from New York to Chicago during a snowstorm.

The Terminal (2004, comedy/drama) Tom Hanks again, this time permanently laid over in an airport.

The circumstances, backstories and subplots change dramatically (and sometimes comedically), but each one speaks to the inherent fear of being unable to get back to where they once belonged. From Dorothy getting stuck in Oz to teens being forced to leave their families in *The Hunger Games*, writers frequently capitalize on the feeling of total helplessness by placing their hero far from home.

Daniel Defoe's original take on *Survivor* is just one of many plotlines we see repeatedly, and there's no shame in taking a great theme and making it original for a new audience.

Ironically, a *Gilligan's Island* movie with a modern-day cast was originally supposed to be made years ago, but it never set sail. Perhaps the professor is still working on his coconut camera.

IT'S ABOUT TIME

At one time or another, we all wish we could go back for a redo. Which could explain the popularity of another oft-visited theme in fiction, time travel.

Recalling Hollywood hits like *Looper* (2012), the idea of Bruce Willis going back 30 years in time and meeting his younger self is intriguing indeed. Demi Moore might even want to see that. And apparently, so did many other folks, as *Looper* brought in $176 million at the box office.

Looper joined a long legacy of films and books in which the hero engages in some form of time-shifting. A few well-known examples include (those with * are based on novels):

The Map of Tiny Perfect Things (2021, romance)*
Teenagers trapped in a time loop create perfect moments together.

About Time (2013, romance)
A young man goes back in time to correct missed opportunities.

Source Code (2011, action) Jake Gyllenhaal is repeatedly sent back to the same 8-minute time frame to thwart a train bombing.

The Time Traveler's Wife (2009, romance)* Eric Bana has no control over his spontaneous time traveling.

13 Going on 30 (2004, romance) Jennifer Garner gets her birthday wish to be all grown up.

Big (1988, comedy) After wishing he weren't so small, a 12-year-old wakes up as 30-year-old Tom Hanks. He can also play piano with his feet.

Peggy Sue Got Married (1986, romance) Kathleen Turner goes back 25 years and reconsiders the choices she made, such as Nicholas Cage.

Back to the Future (1985, adventure) Michael J. Fox and Christopher Lloyd visit 1955, 2015, and 1885 in this renowned trilogy.

Groundhog Day (1983, comedy) Bill Murray is a weatherman stuck in a 24-hour time loop.

Somewhere in Time (1980, romance)* Christopher Reeve falls in love with a girl in an antique photo, and finds a way to meet her in the past.

The Time Machine (1960 and 2002, fantasy)* The 1895 classic that started it all, in which the writer himself travels forward hundreds of thousands of years. Again, H.G. Wells was ahead of his time.

I'd be remiss not to mention one of my favorite books, written by the late Jack Finney. In *Time and Again,* an artist goes back to 1882 and has trouble staying there. At one point, Robert Redford was said to be planning to turn it into a movie, but it never came about. If they ever do make *Time and Again* as a film and it's successful enough to warrant a sequel, Finney was kind enough to provide that too, via a second novel called *From Time to Time.*

Whether it comes under the heading of science fiction, fantasy, or speculation, one notable thing about time travel tale-spinning is that it's one of the few "out there" genres that are accessible enough for anyone, including those who normally avoid science fiction. It's a time-tested trope that always manages to be trendy.

BE A TRAILBLAZER

I once heard a film critic claim that the most important movie of our time is *Star Wars.* Mind you, he was wearing a Jedi tunic at the time, so I suspect his opinion was a tad compromised.

After initially dismissing his declaration, I decided to weigh the evidence. *Star Wars* inarguably spawned its share of imitators, inspired a new generation of filmmakers, and revived science fiction to a popularity it hadn't enjoyed since the '50s. It introduced characters, images, movie quotes, theme music, and special effects that are burned into our collective consciousness as vividly as a light saber.

Not that there aren't other movies just as catalytic. From *The Wizard of Oz* to *Jaws* to *The Hunger Games*, every so often something new comes along that has so much impact on its craft it becomes an instant classic.

We can just as readily spot the milestones of television (*I Love Lucy, Saturday Night Live, Survivor* all were groundbreakers), music (*The Beatles, Michael Jackson, Madonna*), and stage (*The Sound of Music, Cats, Hamilton*). Even beyond their own success and endurance is the clear influence they've had on countless others in their field.

But let's talk books. Who are the literary equivalents of these pioneers? Who are the authors whose work has made such a difference that the world of books would not be the same without them?

We look at these authors as if they're untouchable gods of literature to whose level of greatness we could never hope to come near, but in truth they were no different from you and me. They had something to say, so they wrote it down. Did they have any idea at the time that they would change everything? Not likely. But they probably felt the same spark we get when a good idea hits us or we turn a phrase that gives us the momentary thrill of creation.

Is it just possible that the book inside you right now could change the world like *Romeo & Juliet* or *Great Expectations*? I like to think so. Someone is going to be the next great writer. Write as if it's you.

Chapter 3
LESSONS IN UNEXPECTED PLACES

"Originality in nothing but judicious imitation. The most original writers borrowed from one another."

Voltaire

THE SINCEREST FORM OF FLATTERY

As we've seen, inspiration comes in many forms, often while we're exploring ideas from other sources and putting our own spin on them. We honor those who've boldly gone before us by letting their legacy lead us into new territory.

Like the Sorcerer's Apprentice, we can create a little magic of our own by emulating methods used by the masters. With that in mind, here are time-tested takeaways from some longstanding success stories.

LESSONS FROM THE FEUD

Call it mindless entertainment, a cheap thrill, or just a way to kill 30 minutes, but I'll admit I'm one of those who'll stop on the Game Show Network if *Family Feud* is in the middle of Fast Money. I've got to stick around and see if my answers are better than those of the contestants, and of course they are, unfettered as I am by no lights, cameras, or pressure.

But my real motives are far more academic than just a momentary ego boost, as there is much to be learned about our craft of writing when we look into some of the psychology of *Family Feud*.

What we stand to learn from this enduring enterprise—which has been on the air in some capacity or another since 1976—begins with one of the most oft-repeated principles in writing circles:

Show, Don't Tell

Back in the days of its first host, Richard Dawson, there was a lot of non-game gab. In fact, the show was fairly insufferable for the first few minutes as he interviewed each individual contestant, asking where they're from, what they do for a living, how many pets they have, everything short of who they were in a past life.

Doing so was fairly standard game show patter, and I blame it all on Groucho Marx, who started the whole business of interrogating contestants to get them to say the secret word on *You Bet Your Life*.

But that's not the case in this 21st century, as today's audiences won't sit still for long. We're used to music videos, jump cuts, and getting right down to business. We're here for the main course, so show us the money.

As writers, we likewise needn't spell out every single exhaustive detail for the reader. Rather than have a character tell them that he's spent the last ten years hating his job as an accountant, simply show him at work, sweating over a ledger and being forced to stay late by a demanding boss. They'll get it.

How Many Hosts?

Take a guess. How many different hosts has the Feud had over the years? There's Richard Dawson, of course. Ray Combs and Louie Anderson are often overlooked, as they don't seem to show up in reruns. Richard Karn and John O'Hurley came next, and now they have Steve Harvey.

That's six distinctly unique personalities, but the show has always worked, because the time-tested formula remained popular and was never essentially tampered with. We aren't there for the host as much as the game itself, or the plot, if you will.

As we've discussed before, a good plot can be retold again and again under different disguises. *West Side Story* was *Romeo and Juliet* with a fire escape instead of a balcony. Give a proven story a facelift, and the audience embraces the combination of freshness and familiarity.

Good Answer!
"Name a food item that goes bad if it's not refrigerated."
"Umm..."
"Three seconds."
"An apple!"

You have to feel some empathy for the family members, who, after their in-law gives a woefully pathetic response, still muster the ability to clap and say "Good answer!" You can even hear the weak commitment level in their voice. Yet they support their teammate, why? Because friends don't let friends go down in flames on national television.

The lesson to be learned here is that when we're writing, we are not on national television, so those rules don't apply. Rather than seek (or give) false praise over a less than awesome manuscript, the situation calls for genuine feedback from a trusted source that won't just be a pat on the back. Whether it's our critique partner, spouse, agent, or editor, it's everyone's responsibility to help one another make our writing the absolute best it can be.

The world of literature will be better for it, and maybe people will spend more time reading (and less time watching silly game shows).

SEVEN THINGS WRITERS CAN LEARN FROM MARTY McFLY

October 2015 was a milestone month for fans of *Back to the Future*, having reached one of the target dates in Marty and Doc's cinematic adventures. Even now, almost four decades after its 1985 release, the trilogy continues to boast a cult following of DeLorean restorers, cosplay devotees, and less fanatical folk who simply enjoy well-told tales.

With that enduring popularity in mind, I offer seven things

that make the *Back to the Future* series worth a second look for writers.

1. No need for a hero arc

Unlike the typical protagonist, Marty doesn't experience an inner change that makes him grow as a person by the end of the story. Instead, everything around him changes. For the audience, that is satisfying enough. Just like James Bond, Indiana Jones, or Frodo, the hero in a series is pretty much consistent from story to story, while it's the new adventure providing most of the variety.

2. *Back to the Future* wasn't going to be a trilogy

Screenwriter Robert Zemeckis had only intended to make the one movie. Only because of its enormous success did he write two sequels. Had he known up front that that would happen, he says he would have ended the first movie differently: He wouldn't have had Marty's girlfriend get into the time machine. He would have preferred for Marty and Doc Brown to go on their next mission alone. That script complication was dealt with (a little too conveniently) by zapping her with a ray to make her think it was all a dream.

The lesson here is: The End might not be The End, so be forward-thinking just in case you're lucky enough for fans to demand a follow-up.

3. Believable characters

To maintain realism in a fantasy, it helps to anchor it with characters who react like real people. In *Back to the Future*, there are no wild and wacky sidekicks or talking animals to suspend belief. Even the quirky Doc Brown is no more off the wall than your crazy uncle. Each character contains humanity that invites us to invest ourselves in them.

4. Keeping it down to earth

As for the fantastic storyline, Michael J. Fox himself has

made the observation that the radical visionary aspects of *Back to the Future* didn't get too complex. He cited a debate over whether flying cars would need imaginary lanes to drive in since they have the entire sky in which to navigate. But the script didn't get into all that; flying cars are fantastic enough without giving the audience too many intricacies to distract them.

5. Reassuring repetition

Like the *Back to the Future* movie posters that echoed each other, repeating gags and catch phrases from film to film also gave the audience a comforting sense of familiarity. Whenever Biff taunted, "What are you, chicken?", we knew Marty was about to go full McFly.

6. Be flexible

When producers couldn't strike a deal with Crispin Glover to reprise his role as Marty's dad, they brought in another actor and awkwardly tried to fool audiences using prosthetics or showing him upside down. To ease everyone's pain, they eliminated him from the story as soon as possible. Bottom line: If one of your characters is giving you too much trouble, don't try to negotiate; write him out mercilessly.

7. Take advantage of marketing tie-ins

Like cozy mystery authors who offer recipes and other tangible story elements to fans, Pepsi capitalized on one of the iconic series symbols during the film's 30th anniversary. A bottle of Pepsi Perfect, in a collectible container, sold out faster than 88 MPH on October 21st, 2015. Public demand, however, made 6,500 more available and they sold out within ten minutes.

Some laud *Back to the Future* as the best-written trilogy of all time. Bob Zemeckis said he wouldn't attempt a fourth episode lest he do it a disservice. We can take many cues from Marty and friends in our own quest to write a story that stands the test of time.

TEN THINGS WRITERS CAN LEARN FROM FRANKENSTEIN

Mary Wollstonecraft Shelley was only 18 years old when she wrote *Frankenstein: or, The Modern Prometheus*. While she wrote an impressive number of later works including poetry, travelogues, biographies and children's stories, nothing solidified her stance in literature like the story of a boy and his monster.

If you've ever poured your heart and soul into a writing project, you know it can feel like a matter of life and death to make the right words come alive. With props to Mary Shelley, here are tips from the crypt to give your creature life.

1. Find the right bits and pieces

For all his faults, Victor Frankenstein was a discriminating monster maker, selecting only prime cuts. Like a postmortem Paula Deen, he'd be quick to reject, say, a lopsided brain. We must be equally willing to discard a weak plot point or a character who drags our story down.

Meanwhile, we can bravely borrow tidbits of ideas from the vast laboratory of literature that already exists. Be a grave robber if the spirit strikes, and dig up elements of *Treasure Island* or *The Shining* to reanimate.

2. Dream a little dream

Mary Shelley is said to have concocted her outrageous tale in a "waking dream." Whether she was referring to a lucid dream or a daydream, some authors do their best work when they are indeed away from the keyboard. Mulling over ideas while driving, walking, or lying awake at night can provide blessed distance from the cursed cursor.

3. Draw from your own life

Shelley's original classic contains enough death to fill a mausoleum, but so did her personal life. Her mother, her sisters, even her own daughter, had all met with untimely ends, and the women in her book were no more fortunate. Mary's familiarity with the cruel reality of death permeates her pages.

4. Know what size your idea is

Frankenstein was originally going to be a short story, but it was a huge concept that needed room to fully explore its complex implications. Shelley soon recognized it had too much potential to be caged in, and decided to flesh it out.

5. Include a little romance

It will never be confused with *Casablanca,* but like most popular stories, *Frankenstein* contains a smattering of amor to keep the ladies interested. Even the monster communicates his need to be loved and asks the good doctor to sew up a spouse for him.

6. Set a trend

Dracula may claim he's hundreds of years old, but Frankenstein beat him to the marketplace by a good eight decades. *Frankenstein* was the frontrunner of fear, the gruesome grandfather of all monsters to follow. Let us all craft a story so ahead of its time that future generations of writers will be forced to follow in our footsteps. If a rookie of 18 pulled it off, why can't we?

7. Make the unbelievable believable

This tale of messing with the laws of nature is no less science fiction than *The Matrix*. But what makes *Frankenstein* the chiller that it is, is the believability factor. We're not asked to accept alien life forms or devote mental energy to learning the workings of a fictitious world. Instead, we're fed possibilities with some basis in truth. In 1818 scientists had already proven that lifeless human tissue could be reanimated using electricity. It was just a hop, skip and a jump away to accept that a brain could start thinking again, and what might happen if it did.

If we're going to take readers on a fantastic journey, it helps to make sure it's not so far out that they can no longer relate.

8. Engage in friendly competition

Frankenstein wouldn't have been written had Shelley and three of her writing friends not decided to compete to see who could write the best horror story. A little motivation, obviously, can create a monster. Today, writers who participate in National Novel Writing Month or one of the other organized events for writers have found it a fun and communal way to breathe life into a manuscript.

9. Don't listen to critics

Mary Shelley's tale of terror was soundly rejected by the first publishing company that read it. Even after it was published, critics dismissed it, condemning it just as much for the fact that it was written by a young woman as for its horrific subject matter.

You'll do yourself a favor if you accept up front that your creation will be hideous to certain hapless townsfolk, who may seek to torch it. But within a reasonably short time, *Frankenstein* found its audience, and so will you.

10. Think sequel

A subplot in *Frankenstein* gave Universal Pictures enough material to conjure up *The Bride of Frankenstein*, and that was only the beginning. Soon to follow were *Son of Frankenstein*, *The Ghost of Frankenstein, Curse of Frankenstein,* and *House of Frankenstein*. It seems they only stopped short of *International House of Frankenstein*.

The book you're writing right now could well be the beginning of a series. If you've created characters your audience can't get enough of, you don't have to stop at The End. Leave that door partly open and you'll be able to walk right in again.

Writing isn't brain surgery, but we can take a few of these cues from Dr. Frankenstein. If we do, we stand a better chance of being able to step back from our creation and maniacally declare, "It's alive!"

TEN THINGS WRITERS CAN LEARN FROM THE BEAV

It may be before your time, but please indulge me since *Leave It to Beaver* continues to delight audiences via streaming services. If you already happen to be a fan, dare I suggest you'll enjoy the book *Eddie: The Life and Times of America's Preeminent Bad Boy*. Co-authored by Christopher J. Lynch, *Eddie* is the entertaining autobiography of Ken Osmond, in which he relates firsthand his fascinating life in and out of the beloved sitcom. I had the distinct honor of voicing the audiobook and can attest to what a genuinely decent human being the real Eddie Haskell was.

Shameless plugs aside, it would be a fitting tribute to recognize some of the things any writer can benefit from through the TV classic *Leave It to Beaver*.

1. Give your characters a believable setting

The fictional town of Mayfield gained credibility via regular reminders of local landmarks like the malt shop, the fire station, and Friends Lake. *Leave It to Beaver* purposely included more outdoor shots than most other sitcoms of its time. A strong sense of place gives added personality to the story.

2. Find drama in simple things

Nowhere in its run from 1957-1963 do we experience explosions, hostage situations, desperate housewives, etc. The worst we might see is kids hiding an alligator in the bathtub. The innocence of childhood running into itself kept audiences tuning in every week for six years.

3. Create a strong supporting cast

Eddie Haskell. Need I say more?

4. Make your antagonist entertaining

It would be unfair to call Eddie a villain, but his talent for instigating trouble can't be written off, making him TV's most notorious second banana under 21.

5. Write dialogue that fits the character

June, Ward and Ward's coworker Fred Rutherford were age-appropriate and eloquent. Beaver, Wally and their friends, meanwhile, frequently engaged in slangy kidspeak. From "gee whiz" and "crummy" to "rat" and "creep", they were always giving each other the business.

6. Genre-hopping can be fun and profitable

The head writers of *Leave It to Beaver* had previously spent twelve years writing for the Amos and Andy radio show. Many find it ironic that they wrote one of the most controversial radio shows and one of the most white bread TV shows of all time. What both of these had in common was uncommonly brilliant and relatable humor.

7. Write from life

Head writer Joe Connelly drew many of the show's scenarios from his own seven children. He kept notes and jotted down ideas when observing his youngsters with their friends. The episode where Beaver wore a knitted cap in the school photo to hide a butchered haircut? His son did that.

8. Have teachable moments

If teens sneak into a movie theater and get caught, there is retribution. If parents misinterpret their children's good intentions and punish them, apologies are in order. If a kid climbs into a giant coffee cup on a dare, trouble is brewing. Audiences learn the lessons of life from stories that relay a strong moral code of right and wrong, action and consequence.

9. Branch out

Board games, lunchboxes and breakfast cereals were just a few of the merchandising tie-ins the show capitalized on. Many of today's savviest authors offer their fans recipes from their heroine's kitchen, or post video trailers as slick as a movie trailer.

10. Choose your title with care
The show was originally going to be called *Wally and the Beaver*. It got changed when sponsors thought it sounded like a nature program.

Good writing principles never go out of style, and the legacy of Theodore and company can serve us well even six decades later. Humanize the heartbeat of your story with an entertaining reflection of reality, and your own Mayfield will come to life.

And may I say you're looking quite lovely today, Mrs Cleaver.

EIGHT THINGS WRITERS CAN LEARN FROM MARY POPPINS

Richard M. Sherman and his brother Robert B. Sherman may not be household names, but the story songs they wrote are known worldwide via Walt Disney films and parks, including what they considered their crowning glory, *Mary Poppins*. Along with their Oscar-winning score, the Shermans were key players in developing the story structure of this enduring family classic, which has since made it to Broadway.

Let's get magical and musical with eight things all writers can learn from the prolific songwriting team whom Walt himself affectionately referred to as "the boys."

1. Combine ideas
There are eight books in the Mary Poppins series. Scenes and concepts from different books were brought together to create a storyline for the classic 1964 screenplay. Are there any ideas you've put aside that could find a new home in your latest work?

2. Find the real story
The magical English nanny had many colorful adventures, but Richard & Robert determined that these random episodes offered no character arcs and couldn't carry a feature-length

story. They convinced Walt that Mary's employers should be distracted parents who rediscover the joy of childhood along with their children. Once a moral was chosen, the adventures took on a common purpose.

3. Come up with a new twist

For Mary's signature song, the Shermans wanted to give her a clever proverb, like "An apple a day..." or "A stitch in time..." The end result ("A spoonful of sugar helps the medicine go down") was inspired by Robert's young son, whose school had administered a polio vaccine placed on sugar cubes for easier consumption. You never know what phrase you write could become an instant classic.

4. Secondary characters are people too

In the books, Bert was only a minor character, a street artist known as The Match Man. He has much more prominence in the film, and his role as a chimney sweep was borrowed from a different character in the P.L. Travers series. Bert was given a presence and personality strong enough to be a companion for Mary Poppins. His equally charismatic signature song, "Chim Chim Chiree", won the 1965 Oscar for Best Original Song.

5. Pick the right time period

The Shermans moved the story from the depression-era 1930s to the more hopeful turn of the century. Setting the story in 1910 London also allowed them to develop one character into a suffragette. Speaking of whom...

6. Rise to the challenge

Actress Glynis Johns thought she had been cast to play Mary Poppins, only to learn that Julie Andrews had already been signed to the title role. Walt appeased Johns by assuring her that the Shermans had written an especially great song just for her to sing. In truth, it wasn't even a thought up to that point. But Richard and Robert picked up the gauntlet and delivered a big and brassy number ("Sister Suffragette") to give her a chance to shine.

7. Save some things for a rainy day
The Shermans wrote 32 songs for possible inclusion in Mary Poppins, but only 14 were used when Walt declared the rest "unnecessary" for the story. Some were repurposed in later Disney features including *Bedknobs and Broomsticks* and *The Jungle Book*.

8. Close the door
The Sherman brothers avoided distractions like the plague. When it was time to write, they shut out the world around them to concentrate on the project at hand.

In everything they wrote, Richard and Robert believed that story always comes first. By adopting that same focus, we can give our writing a little extra magic that is practically perfect in every way.

WHAT SGT PEPPER CAN TEACH WRITERS
As we speak, The Beatles' monumental 1967 album is enjoying a new Dolby Atmosphere mix and all-star concerts paying tribute to the Summer of Love classic that made the music world's head spin. Sgt. Pepper may have "taught the band to play," but he also provided some teachable moments for writers.

A little friendly competition can be a good thing
Wordsmiths readily draw inspiration from other wordsmiths. The Beatles' *Rubber Soul* album (1965) motivated The Beach Boy's Brian Wilson to create their most ambitious album, *Pet Sounds* (1966). Then, impressed by *Pet Sounds*, Paul McCartney set out to create an album capable of topping that. To this day, both *Sgt. Pepper's Lonely Hearts Club Band* (1967) and *Pet*

Sounds remain in the Top Ten of most reviewers' Greatest Albums of All Time lists.

No filler

Albums traditionally contain only a couple of hit-worthy heavyweights, with less catchy songs comprising the rest of the collection. In order to produce an album that would surpass any before it, the Fab Four were committed to make every song a standout. During these sessions, it became typical for Paul to spend three hours of studio time just capturing the perfect bass track, or for all four to run through a song till dawn trying different tempos and instruments till they found the exact sound they were looking for.

Putting that same painstaking care into every chapter of our book (including the middle that tends to sag) will ensure that the whole is greater than the sum of its parts.

Mixing Fact and Fantasy into Creative Nonfiction

Some of *Sgt. Pepper's* most acclaimed cuts came from real-life influences: an 1843 circus poster in John Lennon's house ("Being for the Benefit of Mr. Kite"); a classmate of his young son ("Lucy in the Sky with Diamonds"); a runaway in a news story ("She's Leaving Home"); a parking ticket left on Paul's car by a meter maid ("Lovely Rita"); the death of a rich acquaintance ("A Day in the Life").

Each time we write, it's a mix of our experience and our imagination. If we have the eyes to see it, everything in life can be a trigger for creativity.

Variety is the spice of life

No other group in history experimented as much as The Beatles, who created many of the innovations that are now staples of the studio. From aural innovations to genre-hopping (pop, rock, psychedelic, vaudeville, classical, Indian music), they refused to settle into the convenient comfort of familiarity. Recording engineer Geoff Emerick learned to never say no to their crazy requests, instead finding a way to make it happen.

Writers who challenge themselves to move forward into uncharted territory are the ones who break new ground.

Establish the mood with the right title

Although *Sgt. Pepper's Lonely Hearts Club Band* is widely considered to be the first "concept album", the only connective elements are the opening medley introducing the fictional singers and a wrap-up near the end as the "band" leaves the stage. Otherwise it's a collection of unrelated songs, not unlike an anthology of short stories. But the distinctive title (inspired by salt and pepper packets on a plane) ties it all together. Strive to make your book title just as memorable.

A little help from a (talented) friend

Perfectionists though they were, the Fab Four benefited from fine tuning. Enter the objective, experienced ear of producer George Martin. His background in classical music, jazz, comedy albums and children's records gave him the unique ability to take anything the lads could throw at him and refine it into a polished production.

Geniuses though we humbly be, we're usually too close to our own writing to see what other people see. Seek the feedback of carefully-chosen first readers as well as an established editor before releasing your latest masterpiece.

TEN THINGS WRITERS CAN LEARN FROM THE BEATLES

That's right, I'm not done with The Beatles. The Fab Four taught us much more about creativity, collaboration, and just plain cool stuff. Here are selected lessons from Liverpool that writers can benefit from eight days a week.

1. They studied their writing heroes

In their first few albums, The Beatles included 23 cover

songs by songwriters and artists they admired, from Chuck Berry to Buddy Holly and even Buck Owens. By following the examples of the masters in their field, they learned the ropes and climbed them to a whole new level.

2. They built a platform

Before they ever showed up on vinyl, they took the long and winding road to stages from Liverpool to Hamburg, making a name for themselves and creating a demand for their product in advance of the product. Youngsters bombarded record stores trying to buy something that didn't even exist yet. If The Beatles were starting out today, you can be sure they'd be all over social media and YouTube.

3. They drew inspiration anywhere it could be found

(No, I don't mean drugs.) You may have heard the story of how "Yesterday" came to Paul in a dream, and how he originally wrote "Hey Jude" for John's son Julian, but that's just the tip of their iconic iceberg. Circus posters, ambulance sirens and wives who wouldn't return phone calls led to some of the most memorable songs in the Beatles catalog.

4. They weren't afraid to experiment

(I'm still not talking about drugs.) Their quest for creativity knew no bounds. They were always pressing producer George Martin to come up with new recording effects and unique instruments to try. Even the sound of Ringo's drum kit was revolutionary because for the first time, microphones were placed close to the drums instead of at a distance. Pop music has been miking drums that way ever since.

From string quartets to sitars, from backwards effects to tape loops, The Beatles introduced things their audience had never heard before. What new tools might you use today?

5. They were tweakers

To hear their meticulously crafted songs, it's hard to imagine the rough first drafts they started out as. But outtakes don't lie, and it's a fascination to hear the sometimes awkward and even sloppy early versions of some of their greatest hits, which sometimes took two dozen or more takes before they were satisfied. Lyrics were especially prone to revision. Lennon's beloved "In My Life" was originally an ode to Liverpool landmarks until he rewrote it as a love song.

6. The Quiet Beatle didn't stay quiet

With frontmen Paul and John writing hit after hit, one might think George Harrison wouldn't even try to compete as a songwriter and potentially invite unfair comparison in this most visible of venues. But he let his talent speak for itself and wrote roughly 1/10th of the Beatles 200+ album songs. His own "Something" remains the second most-covered composition in their catalog behind "Yesterday".

6. They were smart collaborators

Relying on their individual strengths, the songwriting team of Lennon & McCartney was often really just one or the other, with a healthy dose of influence from the silent partner. Legend has it that Paul kept John from getting too hard, and John kept Paul from getting too soft. Other times they would both come in with an unfinished song and then put them together to create a complete composition. They were also not opposed to enlisting a little help from their friends, like Eric Clapton, who plays one of the most famous guitar solos on the White Album.

7. They knew when to change course

That is, they recognized when spending too much time touring was cutting into the creative process. When they performed their last concert in 1966, the goal was to spend more time writing and recording, which they did. Several years later, when artistic differences got in the way, they broke up. They could have hung up their hats while they were on top, but instead each embarked on successful solo careers. Worth pointing out also is that John later took five years off when he decided it was more important to just be with his family.

8. They had great covers

The Beatles invited you to judge a record by its cover, via some of the most imitated album art in history. How many people have had their picture taken walking across Abbey Road? And the cover of *Sgt Pepper's Lonely Hearts Club Band* attracted more analytic attention than virtually any album before or since. Of course, they didn't create these covers themselves. They had the pros do it.

9. They paid it forward

After achieving success of their own, they found and fostered others with budding talent, most notably Mary Hopkin ("Those Were the Days"), Badfinger ("Come and Get It"), Billy Preston ("Will It Go 'Round in Circles") and James Taylor (too many to count). Each of them started out on the Beatles' Apple label.

10. All you need is love

Writers who don't write typically blame it on not having enough talent or time, or because they think they won't succeed. Writers who *do* write do it because they love writing so much that they have no choice. Fame and fortune can be great motivators, but true success comes to those who do what they love and love what they do. These are the folks who go from being a nowhere man to a paperback writer. For them, happiness is a warm pen.

Chapter 4
GETTING WORDY

"The difference between the almost right word and the right word is really a large matter—'tis the difference between the lightning-bug and the lightning."

Mark Twain

With a ready supply of brainstorming triggers under our belt, it's time to think about turning our brilliant ideas waiting to get out into tangible works of genius. Let's begin by considering the most essential elements of what we have to work with—namely, the words themselves.

THE SYMPHONY OF SYLLABLES

Music lover that I am, one of my favorite getaways is to go to the symphony. I'll never cease to be amazed by the astounding feat of eighty musicians all striking up the band at the wave of a baton and staying in perfect sync for two hours amid a myriad of ever-changing nuances and tempos. There's also something about live orchestral music—definitely its lack of words for one thing—that allows one to become thoroughly enveloped in the musical experience.

Even while under the rapture of Rachmaninoff, the wordsmith in me is still present and accounted for, and I can't help analyzing how the art of music can be very much like the art of writing. They really have a great deal in common.

Majors & Minors

A song with predominantly major chords (such as *Do-Re-Mi*) tends to sound positive, happy, hopeful, while a song in mostly minors (*The Funeral March*) evokes gloom, misery, danger.

Highs & Lows
We think of high sounds as bright and illuminating, while low, deep tones sound dark, even claustrophobic.

Tempo
Fast passages suggest busy activity and forward motion, while slow passages evoke introspection and ponderance.

Volume
Loud feels boisterous, triumphant, powerful! Quiet feels caring, tentative, gentle.

What does all of this have to do with words? The same principles apply to every sentence we write. Our choice of words has a huge bearing on the mood of the moment. Compare these simple sentences, for example:

1. "Will you let Livia know Wednesday is good for dinner?"
2. "Take this pan to Teresa and tell her Tuesday is potluck."

Number two has a little more punch because it's packed full of plosives (Ts and Ps). Even if we don't read it aloud, our brain reacts to all those little percussive power points.

If you're trying to further a particular mood (Aggressive? Easygoing?) your choice of soft or hard words can lend its own subliminal slant. Likewise, the structure and syntax of your prose can provide a smooth, rhythmic flow or an intentionally unstable one.

And sometimes less is more. Which of these two statements get your attention?

1. I'm telling you, if you do that again, I will never forgive you as long as I live.
2. Don't. Just don't.

I think most of us would heed the second one.

And a great classical work has multiple movements. Let me belabor this for one more second to make an important point.

A typical progression in a symphony consists of Allegro (lively), Adagio (slower), Scherzo (swift), and back to an Allegro finale, bigger than before. Isn't this very much like every story, in which we start with an inviting premise, then we give the hero problems to bog them down, then they find the strength to answer the call of battle, until finally they wave the flag of victory? That's when we break out the timpani for some heavy duty fireworks. Throughout all of this, we provide a roller coaster of ups and downs, fast and slow, and hard and soft to keep things from getting monotonous.

Every sentence we compose is part of a symphony, bigger than the sum of its parts. Each measure of our composition will measure up if we put the right mood into the words we choose. With over 250,000 words in the English language, we have a lot of notes to play with.

SPECIFICALLY SPEAKING

It happens more often than we'd like to admit. From time to time in our writing, it's inevitable that we will include pet words which we tend to overuse. Our spoken conversations with friends are harmlessly sprinkled with these intrusive little nuisances, but when they become apparent in our writing, it can be downright embarrassing.

Medical thriller author Dr Richard Mabry shared this experience after getting his first contract. His novel was accepted, but his editor pointed out that he must be in love with the word "just". The editor, who had seen examples of this practice among writers time and again explained, "All of us have pet words or phrases, and we tend to employ the same constructions in our sentence structure. Mix it up." Dr Mabry took umbrage at this until he did a word search and, sure enough, his manuscript was peppered with incidents of "just". His resulting rewrite and removal of additional favorite words resulted in a story that was cleaner and easier to read, revealed the award-winning author.

One important side of this coin of commonly coined words involves the intrinsic value of the pet word itself. I can't tell you how many debates I've been party to in which an editor friend decried the use of "that" when it's out of place or just plain unnecessary, as in "I think that she's right." I do think she's right about that.

And I often recall an incident with John Lennon in which he and Paul McCartney were writing the lyrics to "With a Little Help from My Friends". He was struggling to come up with a good line to rhyme with "time". His then-wife Cynthia suggested, "How about 'I just feel fine'?" Her offering was promptly shot down by Lennon, who criticized the word "just" as being a pointless word having no meaning.

Of course, in the right context, "just" has purpose, like when establishing the timing of something. "I just got back from the store" is more descriptive than "I got back from the store." But John had a point in that "I just feel fine" is essentially the same as "I feel fine." Ironically, several years later, he would write the line "...I just don't know how to feel" ("How", 1971).

I myself will admit to a certain affinity for the word "great", which I'm trying to stop using. Not because it lacks meaning, but because it's not specific. If someone tells you your book is "great", what information does that really give you? Yes, they liked it, and that's about it. However, if they say your book is "thought-provoking", "inspired" or "worthy of Twain", you have more than just generic feedback to take to the bank.

We do well to look at the words we tend to overuse in light of their actual value. Eliminate unnecessary words, but also replace general ones with something specific. If we can do that, that would be just great.

SPACE INVADERS

Comedian, producer and author Jerry Seinfeld knows a few

things about communication, and he's shared some interesting insights over the years. One of his more thought-provoking quotes once appeared in a *Parade* interview:

"You have to invade the space of the audience a little bit. I learned that early on. It was a very helpful thing to learn. You have to invade them just a little bit. Not too much, because then it's obnoxious. But you can't be short of them either, or you won't control them."

Invading their space. What does that mean? To a standup comedian it can mean the difference between a standing ovation and getting heckled off the stage. A master performer knows one has to be bigger than life to take ownership of the room and keep all eyes on them. Singers and musicians are especially known for exaggeration and a flashy presence.

But when it's just you standing there talking to an audience—as in public speaking—mastery of volume is one critical skill to develop, as Jerry explains:

"The volume at which I'm speaking now is the right volume for where you're sitting. I'm almost performing, in a way. There's this kind of voice, and then there's this kind of voice, and then there's this kind of voice. I wasn't a natural performer at all, so I learned. I was always a pretty good writer in the beginning, but I really had to learn how to perform."

Communicating through writing is a lot like doing standup. It's just you, the lone voice, trying to reach a vast audience whose faces you can't even see in the dark. You can only rely on their feedback to tell you if you've hit the mark. Jerry's voice of experience provides us with some food for thought:

Invade their space — Go beyond your comfort zone and enter into theirs, with ideas that challenge them and can't be ignored.

"There's this kind of voice" — Determine the most effective "voice" to reach your audience. Not too soft and mushy, not too loud and preachy, but just a bit above the communication level they're used to.

Listen for their feedback — Social media is the modern equivalent of the old audience applause meter, which would determine winners on game shows. Blogging and other online promotion is how savvy authors build an interactive, loyal following.

They say standup comedy is one of the hardest professions in entertainment. I say writers are no slouch either.

AND YOU CAN MISQUOTE ME ON THAT

Okay, film buffs. Which of the following famous movie lines is misquoted?

"Me Tarzan, you Jane."
"You dirty rat; you killed my brother."
"Play it again, Sam."
"I'm ready for my close-up, Mr. DeMille."
"Luke, I am your father."
"If you build it; they will come."

As you may already be aware, they are *all* inaccurate. Despite their familiarity, none of these phrases were ever spoken in those exact words. Close, perhaps, but no cigar.

Ready for a couple more? These come from the pages of literature:

"Elementary, my dear Watson." (Sir Arthur Conan Doyle never penned this, though Sherlock did finally say it in a movie.)
"Money is the root of all evil." (Without its original intro "The *love* of money", its meaning is completely altered.)

Inaccuracy notwithstanding, time and repetition have made classics of these phrases. I would guess a fair share of the movie misquotes are the result of impressionists turning a phrase which becomes the new standard. Most of us remember comics on Johnny Carson delivering a shifty-shouldered, "You dirty rat". And the much wordier "Play it, Sam. Play 'As Time Goes By'; you played it for her, you can play it for me!" simply wouldn't have played the same in front of a Tonight Show crowd.

Despite the occasionally tattered retelling, these are only a handful of the countless quotes which have stood the test of time to become part of our vocabulary. Does it ever make you wonder if the author had any idea it would become a legendary line as they were writing it? Can you imagine the thrill of having a moment when you're crafting dialogue and thinking, "Wow, that's a line that will go down in history"? I know that's an offer I couldn't refuse.

The phrase that pays is as different as each movie itself. The following have nothing in common other than they reveal a huge revelation in the plot:

"I see dead people."
"Houston, we have a problem."
"It's alive! It's alive!"
"You're gonna need a bigger boat."
"Go ahead…make my day."
"You can't handle the truth!"

We can never predict what words are going to click with the public, but it is apparent that movie lines which do become classics are typically uttered by charismatic main characters; heroes and villains whom readers believe are capable of expressing the wisdom of the ages. (With the possible exception of the unnamed lady diner in *When Harry Met Sally* who said, "I'll have what she's having." You must admit, though, she was pretty charismatic in her own right.)

Only time will tell if the protagonist in our novel will deliver the next famous quote. But it does behoove us to give each line of dialogue more than a passing consideration. When putting what might become classic words together, it may help to remember that keeping it short and sweet could be the beginning of a beautiful friendship.

THE PHRASE THAT PAYS
"Live long and prosper."
"Yabba Dabba Doo!"
"De plane! De plane!"

Chances are, these famous lines effortlessly brought up images of Mr Spock, Fred Flintstone and Tattoo, even if it's been decades since you last heard them. From the earliest days of entertainment, the catch phrase has been a staple of dialogue for popular characters. From Fonzie's thumbs-upped "Ayyyy!" to Lucy's toothy "Ewwww," we find reassurance in their familiarity and are disappointed if we don't hear them.

Today the catch phrase remains as popular as ever. "The tribe has spoken," "You are the weakest link," and "Is that your final answer?" entered our modern lexicon through reality and game shows. Likewise, sitcoms and dramas continue to feature main or secondary characters known for repeating pet expressions.

The characters we write can likewise benefit from this verbal quirk. We ourselves have a habit of saying certain phrases, so why not give your protagonist the same liberty? Some of literature's most beloved characters weren't slow to indulge in slogans. The potential of a good catch phrase to weave its way into our hearts is elementary, my dear Watson.

One thing to be careful of is to avoid having more than one character use the chosen phrase. If your hero has a penchant for saying "Holy moly!" it dilutes its power and confuses the reader if the next door neighbor claims it too. That is, unless he or she is purposely echoing it.

Like anything, catch phrases can be overdone to the point of irritation. But tastefully timed appearances are a welcome insider's wink to our readers, offering easy reinforcement of a character's unique personality.

Who knows? Maybe your hero will utter the next catch phrase that will catch on.

TIMING IS EVERYTHING

A funny friend of mine used to love to say this joke:

"The most important thing when you're doing comedy is ... uh ... er ... *timing!*"

Well, it was funny when he said it.

The inherent wisdom behind his witticism was that getting the timing wrong throws things off-kilter. This isn't only true for punchlines, but for any kind of communication. Perhaps even more so when it's the written word. Consider this passage:

> Dan didn't know why he was waking up in a hospital bed. One of the last things he remembered was talking to Eleanor and Benjamin at the party. He looked at his watch. Almost 8. He was in the mood for one more drink before he said goodnight. Suddenly, a nurse appeared at the doorway.

If you were confused reading that, I was just as confused writing it. Was Dan checking his watch at the party or at the hospital? Did a nurse suddenly show up at the party? It all becomes clear in context, but the reader isn't supposed to have to work that hard to sort it out.

Another example of off-timing is when mixing past and present tense:

As the plane takes off, James realized his briefcase is back home on the dining room table. In it were the wood samples that his entire presentation depends on. It will require some clever ad-libbing to describe the different finishes he told Mr Shaw are almost ready.

That blatant example of time-shifting falls all over itself with back and forth ambiguity. In actual practice, opposing tenses tend to creep in much more subtly and stealthily, especially during dialogue segments. Be on guard for "he said" and "he says" that try to share the same time frame.

Another time element that confuses many is the use of "was" versus "were" in statements such as:

"I wish I was homeward bound." (Simon & Garfunkel, 1966)
"I wish I were an Oscar Meyer Weiner." (TV commercial, 1965)

Only one of these is correct. Which one is it?

In matters of non-reality, such as a wish or other imagining, past tense verbs like "were" are the right choice, removing it from the realm of possibility. No one would say, "I were homeward bound," but a sentence that includes "I was" could be taken incompletely to suggest "I was an Oscar Meyer wiener." So songs like "If I Were a Carpenter" were correctly titled, while "If I Was Your Woman" wasn't.

These common mistakes in time and tense are easy to make, but just as easy to fix. Developing good timing will help ensure that your writing is clear and linear and that both you and your reader have a good time.

SECTION II

COMPELLING STORYTELLING

Chapter 5
THE SEQUENCE OF EVENTS

"Sometimes reality is too complex. Stories give it form."
Jean Luc Godard

EASY AS 1 - 2 - 3

The three-act structure is the standard framework in storytelling, going all the way back to Artistotle. Perhaps you've heard it described this way:

    Act 1: Put your hero up a tree
    Act 2: Throw rocks at him
    Act 3: Bring him down

If you're a writer who's been on Facebook or YouTube in recent years, you've probably been presented with a video ad for Ron Howard's Master Class on Directing. In the promo, he refers to a theory held by some that there are "seven stories". They're worth taking a look at, as your story is likely to bear some correlation to one of these themes from which most tales spring forth.

Christopher Booker is credited for writing the book on the subject, namely *The Seven Basic Plots: Why we tell stories.* At around 700 pages, Booker's volume is a thorough analysis of each story line, breaking each down into their own set of stages. For the sake of our immediate purposes, here is an oversimplification:

Overcoming the Monster
Not always a literal monster, but a major threat to our hero, who takes up the challenge to destroy it.

Rags to Riches
An underdog overcomes the odds to become top dog.

The Quest
Our hero must find a treasure of great value, and embarks on a journey to find it.

Voyage and Return
Our hero lands in a place unlike home and must learn new rules to prevail. Eventually he/she returns home better than before.

Comedy
A goal is impeded by funny obstacles. Often, if the main obstacle is a person, they get a come-uppance in the end.

Tragedy
Our hero is his own worst enemy, with qualities that lead to his downfall.

Rebirth
The ultimate character arc, in which the hero transforms into a new being, literally or figuratively.

In reading these, you may have already thought of stories that contain more than one of these plots. For example, isn't *The Wizard of Oz* a voyage to a strange world as well as a treasure quest?

Booker himself acknowledges the frequent overlap of plots, and adds two more which he considers less common:

Rebellion
The hero rebels but ultimately surrenders to—and perhaps joins—the powers that be.

Mystery
The hero seeks to discover the truth of a murder or other unexplained event.

Some writers feel that lumping stories into categorized plots is disrespecting their originality. Others feel that there are as many as 25 plots, not merely seven. For his part, Ron Howard implies that there is just one, but we may have to buy his Master Class to learn what that is.

In his classic book *Story*, legendary screenwriting expert Robert McKee declares: "A rule says *you must do it this way*. A principle says *this works, and has through all remembered time*." Why reinvent the wheel from scratch when someone has already rounded out the edges for you?

The fact that we can think of our favorite movies or books and see how they fit into one or more of these story lines is testament to their enduring effectiveness and popularity. Could you possibly insert your hero's name into one of the seven plots and refine it into the logline for your next novel? Your own creativity will make the time-tested tale uniquely yours.

PLOTTING LIKE A VIEW-MASTER

It's been a long time since I hung out in the toy department, but on a recent visit I was surprised to see that one of my childhood favorites was still around. Perhaps at some point you too owned a View-Master.

This plastic viewer, held up to the eyes like binoculars, let you experience genuine 3D images. Depending on which disc you inserted, you could see stereoscopic views of everything from the Grand Canyon to TV shows. Grimm's Fairy Tales and Disney stories were among the more popular titles.

As you manually advanced to each of the seven scenes on a disc, a tiny window displayed a few words describing what you were seeing. View-Master discs told many popular tales in this condensed format. Which meant that *an entire story had to be told in seven scenes.*

Does that tell you something? What it suggests to me is that a story can be broken down and told in as few as seven beats.

Apparently the View-Master isn't alone in thinking this way. Numerous writing resources spell out classic seven-point outlines. There are variations, but here's a common breakdown:

1. The Beginning

A setup that establishes the character in his/her current circumstances.

2. Plot Point 1

An inciting event, a catalyst that changes the status quo.

3. Pinch Point 1

A personal challenge that requires the hero to take action.

4. Mid-Point

At this point of no return, the hero is fully committed and proactively tries to fix things.

5. Pinch Point 2

The hero fails. At this low point an additional crisis makes it appear that all is lost.

6. Plot Point 2

The final confrontation with the antagonist. Most of the time, the hero will prevail.

7. Ending

This satisfying epilogue reveals how things are in the new normal.

In an 80,000-word novel, that translates to roughly 11,400 words for each point. But if you break your story down to its most impactful events, you could convey it in a one-minute summary suitable for an elevator pitch or a workable outline for whatever novel you're working on.

Granted, a picture is worth a thousand words—and the View-Master showed seven of them—but the brief text that accompanied each slide told the same story in the sparsest words possible. When plotting your story, think like a View-Master and you can stir your reader's imagination in vivid 3D.

WHERE DO I BEGIN?

You have an awesome idea for a novel. You may even know how it should end. Sometimes, the trickier part is knowing how you should begin the whole thing. With that in mind, here are three typical story openers which have stood the test of time.

The Catch Up

Think of this as "Once upon a time" or "A long time ago in a galaxy far, far away." Fairy tales and sci-fi frequently rely on this approach when a degree of backstory is necessary for the audience to understand what's about to happen. Why is the queen jealous of Snow White? Why are there star wars? We get the info we need right up front.

When using this approach, be careful not to overload the first chapter with voluminous details to learn. Readers exhaust quickly if they're required to sort out too much information. Instead, ease into unfamiliar territory with the grace of Suzanne Collins. While there is much to learn about the dystopian world of the future, *The Hunger Games* filters in explanations of reapings and District 12 painlessly, alongside an identifiable story that keeps moving.

The Set Up

This approach establishes, at the outset, our hero in his/her current state (their "Ordinary World", as it's called). We'll see them going about their normal routine in their everyday circumstances so that we understand the status quo. After that, things go topsy-turvy and the hero's world as they know it comes under siege by whatever problems the story dictates. A series of ups and downs follows, until finally there is victory and we are rewarded with some scenario that harkens us back to the original roots of the hero.

Establishing the hero's current (i.e. "normal") circumstances before they are thrown into chaos is among the most popular story openers. It's a plus if it offers a glimpse of what they lack in life, getting your character arc off and running. Julie Andrews serenading us on a Swiss mountaintop isn't the only one who can express her heart's desire in her first scene.

The opening chapter is prime time for interaction with supporting characters, which can convey the hero's personality and motivations more readily than a solo scene. Take care, however, to have enough that is interesting afoot so things don't get bogged down in banality. The audience wants to know and empathize with the characters, but they're also eager for something to happen.

Fire 'Em Up

Even before the opening credits, James Bond knows that some audiences like to be shaken, not stirred. The chase is on and no time is wasted getting the action underway. *Raiders of the Lost Ark, Jaws* and countless other action sagas have grabbed attention from the get-go by jumping right into an inciting scene.

In the case of James Bond, we already know 007 chases bad guys, so there is no backstory needed before the thrills begin. However, if your story stars unfamiliar characters, you'll want to introduce them somewhat before throwing them into the furnace. Otherwise, the audience—which has no investment in these people yet—has little reason to care what happens to any of them.

THE OPENING NUMBER

A strong beginning gives the reader a taste of what lies ahead. This can be done in a number of ways, such as starting out with action (like the discovery of a murder in a mystery), or introducing a compelling hero and their present circumstances, soon to be challenged. Additionally, the opening scene will establish the theme or moral that comprises the main idea behind the story.

Let's look at a few examples in depth:

Jaws doesn't fool around. From the opening credits we're plunged under the sea, following the antagonist's own predatory path to the tune of that ominous theme. Already feeling dread, we then see the prey: young people enjoying a beach bonfire, unaware that their party will be crashed in less than five minutes by a great white shark. You might say that the opening of *Jaws* has *teeth*. (Or, if you prefer, *legs*.)

Raiders of the Lost Ark opens with a bite as well, taking you on a relentless thrill ride through death traps, savages and snakes. By the time we observe Indiana Jones at his day job of soft-spoken professor, we're already familiar with his courage, ingenuity and weaknesses because of the riveting opening sequence. It's obvious there'll be more adventure ahead.

The Lord of the Rings begins as classic fairy tales do, by spelling out the backstory up front. We immediately learn of the rings' origin and how they sparked a war between good and evil, just as the Brothers Grimm caught us up on evil stepsisters at the start of Cinderella.

Disney is particularly adept at the opening number. After a typical fairy tale prologue in *Beauty and the Beast*, Belle reveals her hopes and dreams in song while introducing us to her village. The townsfolk chime in with their own observations about the heroine. In the midst of this colorful gaiety, geese fly overhead, and one of them is shot from the sky, giving us an instant negative impression of the man wielding the musket. We've declared him the bad guy even before he has his first conversation with Belle.

Fiddler on the Roof, aided by an introductory narrative from its protagonist, begins with "Tradition", a proud declaration of the code his village lives by, which for the next three hours is threatened at every turn. Pick *any* musical, and the opening number sets the stage for what follows.

Setup is everything. Captivate your audience with a great opening scene, and they're likely to come along for the ride.

YOU ARE HERE

If you've ever gone into an unfamiliar shopping mall trying to find a particular store, you know the feeling. An endless maze of shops and kiosks clamor for your attention and you hardly know where to begin. But before you can say "Where am I?" you spot the friendly sight of the mall directory and search for the reassuring red arrow that tells you "You are here."

It's no accident that the directory is always parked near the entrance door, so shoppers have an opportunity to get their bearing right away.

Similarly, consider the opening shot in any film you've seen. From the very beginning, the first thing you see tells you where you are. It can be as obvious as an airport terminal or as subtle as a closeup on a bathroom faucet. Before you learn anything about "who," "what," or "when", the first thing your mind goes searching for is "where". Once we know where we are, we're no longer geographically disoriented.

When reading a book, we have no such visual cue to establish our whereabouts. Thoughtfully, the classics of literature provide readers with that information very early on.

Consider these opening lines from famous novels:

"Amerigo Bonasera sat in New York Criminal Court Number 3 and waited for justice…"

—Mario Puzo, *The Godfather*

"Renowned curator Jacque Saunière staggered through the vaulted archway of the museum's Grand Gallery."

—Dan Brown, *The Da Vinci Code*

"At the beginning of July, during a spell of exceptionally hot weather, towards evening, a certain young man came down on the street from the little room he rented…"

—Fyodor Dostoevsky, *Crime and Punishment*

"He was an old man who fished alone in a skiff in the Gulf Stream…"

—Ernest Hemingway, *The Old Man and the Sea*

"Mr. and Mrs. Dursley, of number four, Privet Drive, were proud to say they were perfectly normal…"

—J.K. Rowling, *Harry Potter and the Philosopher's Stone*

"Mr. Sherlock Holmes, who was usually very late in the mornings, save upon those not infrequent occasions when he stayed up all night, was seated at the breakfast table."

—Sir Arthur Conan Doyle, *The Hound of the Baskervilles*

(Sir Arthur liked getting *who*, *what*, *when* and *where* out of the way very quickly.)

This is not to suggest that the first sentence always has to declare "where". "Call me Ishmael" (*Moby Dick*) and "It was the best of times, it was the worst of times" (*A Tale of Two Cities*) had other business to get out of the way. But within moments you do discover your whereabouts.

When we're dreaming up our own scenarios, we are intimately attuned to our characters, their actions and their dialogue. We have vivid images of all that. The location, however, can often seem merely incidental to us; almost a nuisance to have to include. But the reader needs that comforting sense of place early on, as well as anytime the scene changes. All those establishing shots in movies answer what would otherwise be a continually nagging question. We never have to even think about where we are. But we definitely would if we hadn't been shown already.

Admittedly, having to come up with something interesting to write in order to acknowledge each changing scene isn't nearly as fun as describing the characters' personalities or penning their clever patter. But your readers will appreciate that nod of consideration. They will be right there in the scene with you if you give them the mile markers that point to the starting gate.

CATALYST ON A HOT TIN ROOF

One of the most intriguing parts of any tale is the inciting incident. That turning point—when the main situation of the plot is set into motion—is when we find ourselves committed to the story to see how things are going to play out.

By now we've been introduced to the characters and their ordinary circumstances. Then, just as we've gotten acclimated, along comes the catalyst that turns everything upside down.

In *Back to the Future*, that moment comes when Marty escapes terrorists by speeding away in Doc Brown's time machine and finds himself transported back to 1955.

In most cases, the inciting incident is something that happens *to* the hero, not something he or she causes. Even in *The Hunger Games*, when Katniss makes the decision to take her sister's place in the deadly contest, it is because she is forced by her own sense of duty to do so.

In a romantic tale, multiple events will come along to complicate things, but it's the moment the future lovebirds first lay eyes on each other that can usually be considered the one that turns everything topsy-turvy.

The "call to adventure", as it's known, will take our hero out of his or her comfort zone and disrupt their world. It doesn't necessarily have to be a tragedy like getting fired or losing a loved one. It can be a good thing like winning the lottery or inheriting a vineyard in Italy. Difficulties will ensue soon enough.

At what point in the story should that dividing line be placed? Professional plotters generally agree that this catalytic converter should occur during the first quarter. For example, in *Back to the Future*, it happens at exactly the ¼ mark, 30 minutes into the two-hour movie. In *The Hunger Games*, it occurs only 15 minutes into the 2 ½ hour flick.

In a different kind of example, the Oscar winner *American Beauty* centers around Lester's midlife crisis, which is triggered by more than one thing, including a dead-end job and a cheating wife. But the pivotal moment comes when he attends a school event and becomes enamored with his daughter's friend. Everything prior is setup. That inciting incident, for the record, takes place 15 minutes into the two-hour film.

Basically, the inciting incident is the event without which the main story cannot happen. Doc Brown can invent a time machine, hunger games will take place no matter what, and Lester's unsatisfying life is already underway, but without these other key moments, the main crisis will not be inflicted upon the hero.

The most effective inciting incident will grip the audience's curiosity as to how the hero will navigate the new situation. At the very least, it will set the stage for even bigger crises to increase the dramatics later.

Very often, that call to adventure is something the hero is going to resist. He has his doubts. He doesn't know if he can handle this. It's a whole new world for him, and he is afraid. Maybe he likes where he is just fine. He doesn't want to go off into the special circumstance.

So there will be some resistance, but eventually something will happen that will force him to enter that special world and get going on this new adventure. After all, what's the point of the story if there's no adventure to jump into?

Done right, this turning point will not only ignite the TNT of your story, but will become the no-turning-back moment for your reader too.

DISCOVERING THE NEW WORLD

Faced with this new challenge, our hero will soon leave his/her comfortable routine and step into the unknown. In Hero's Journey jargon, they "cross the threshold", the dividing line between the ordinary world and the special world.

A vivid example from film is that moment in *The Wizard of Oz* when Dorothy opens the door and suddenly her black and white world becomes Technicolor. It's abundantly clear that we're in a different reality now. Or *Jurassic Park*, in that stunning scene where the paleontologists first arrive and are awed by the sight of a giant brachiosaurus high above them, eating leaves from the trees.

Such startling images are a powerful line of demarcation for our story. But the scene could also be as commonplace as the first day at a new job or beginning a new skill. Our hero might be taking a plane to Italy, or a train to Hogwarts. There are many ways to convey that they're leaving the ordinary world and entering unexplored territory.

As they learn the ropes in this new realm, they will make friends and enemies, and their developing skills will be tested. This middle portion of the story—which traditionally comprises half of it—is what Blake Snyder calls the "fun and games" portion. This is where you play out the promise of the premise.

This is exactly what the reader came for. They want to witness what's going to happen to the hero in this situation. Well, here's where we explore that. We're going to show all the different things that can happen as someone learns how to run a vineyard, or as they train to become a sorcerer at Hogwarts.

This is the hero's initiation stage. They're going to have to learn ways that they can overcome the challenges that are thrown at them, to dramatic or humorous effect. You really can have a lot of fun with this.

The initiation stage is a prime opportunity to explore the mindset of the hero and reveal their motivations, strengths and weaknesses. Slipping in some subtle hints of things to come will also pay off big time when things come full circle.

In *Raiders of the Lost Ark* we learn early on that Indy, an intrepid adventurer, is afraid of snakes. Later in the story, when he is trapped in a temple filled with serpents, we are fully aware of his fear. Strategic foreshadowing is a nice touch worth incorporating into this fun and games segment.

CAUSING TROUBLE

Normal people don't go around looking for trouble. In fact, they do their best to avoid it. More often than not, trouble finds them instead. A flat tire, a power outage, a computer crash—no one anticipates calamity, much less extends an invitation to it.

But when conjuring up a story, mayhem is a welcome guest.

Conflict gives fiction its fire, so we can put our natural human instinct for self-preservation aside and actively invoke troubled times, at least for our main character. The better the obstacles between them and their goal, the more compelling the story.

Since trouble comes in many different flavors, the genre will often dictate the appropriate realm of ruin to choose from. A lover's quarrel that would send Bridget Jones running to her diary is unlikely to hound Sherlock Holmes while investigating a

Baskerville murder. Deciphering whether alien messages are friendly or are declarations of intergalactic war would probably be too intense for a children's book.

Indeed, the age and life circumstances of the intended reader is a ready yardstick for measuring the severity of impending doom. Dealing with a school bully is sufficient drama for a student reader, while a mature audience is capable of pondering the end of mankind. If your protagonist is the approximate age of your typical reader, it's easy to throw the appropriate curveballs their way and have them struggle authentically.

The most tried-and-true formula involves an antagonist who seeks an outcome opposite to that of our hero. The murderer will do everything in his power to prevent being captured. The handsome rancher whom the heroine falls for has vowed never to love again. A cut-throat coworker connives to steal the big promotion away from our hero.

As we know, making trouble for our protagonists is simply a matter of giving them a goal and then putting roadblocks in their way. We can think of our storyline as a maze, where the hero/heroine knows where they need to go, but getting there is just one problem after another thanks to all of their impending obstacles.

"The trouble with trouble," it's been said, "is that it always starts out as fun." Have fun being the real troublemaker in your story. It's the one time you don't have to worry about getting yourself into trouble.

THE OTHER FACES OF CONFLICT

When we think of antagonists from literature, we typically think of the classic villains like Captain Hook, Injun Joe, The Wicked Witch of the West, Hannibal Lecter, Dracula, and the other memorable personifications of evil. But there are many other faces of conflict not of the human variety that can be put to good use in our story.

Many children's books choose not to pit the hero against

another person. Instead, the dilemma comes from a small difficulty that can be turned into a life lesson. A terrific example is *Pete the Cat*, who loves his white shoes. When he steps in strawberries that turn his shoes red, what follows is a simple but brilliant story about learning to accept and love yourself, cleverly disguised as a tale about shoes.

Even as adults, conflict in story teaches us to deal with life, each dilemma in its own small way representing the eternal struggle. A problem is a problem, no matter what form it takes. Here are some classic inhuman antagonists:

Man vs Beast

What's worse than someone you can't even reason with? How about someone that wants to eat you? Ask the heroes of *Jaws* if their adversary doesn't pose a threat.

The irony is that the shark isn't fishing for trouble; he's just doing what comes naturally 'cause it's feeding time. Likewise, the great white whale in *Moby Dick* may or may not understand Captain Ahab's concept of revenge, but it knows all about self-preservation.

The Great Outdoors

Stephen King's *The Girl Who Loved Tom Gordon* is one of many examples of a protagonist trying to survive in the wilderness. Again, there is irony in the fact that a forest, waterfall, mountain, etc mean no harm; they don't even have a conscience. But it's a jungle out there, and a babe in the woods means we're dealing with basic human survival.

Add a tornado or a tempest, and they will stir up plenty of additional trouble. *The Perfect Storm*, *Earthquake* and *Twister* are cinematic examples of how Mother Nature can be a real shrew.

Hard Times

Nellie Olsen wasn't the only thorn in Laura Ingalls' side in her *Little House on the Prairie* books. Tales set in the Old West are particularly filled with the struggle just to make it through life under primitive or poverty-stricken conditions. Mix in some of the previous elements like a grizzly bear, or a drought during growing season, and you have a multi-layered prairie of pain.

Conflict in Nonfiction

Even when we're writing nonfiction, it's not hard to find. My short story "Family Tree" in *Stories of Music, Volume 2* is primarily a retrospective of the musical family I grew up in. I wasn't consciously seeking a way to add drama to this slice of my life; it just happened organically because it was a tragedy that put a stop to the musical collaboration in my family, and, ironically, another tragedy is what brought it all back with new harmony.

A good guy facing off against a bad guy is classic drama. But fighting off the challenges of everyday life are also readily available story helpers to add realistic conflict, often making it even more personal for our hero.

READERS ARE RUBBERNECKERS

While driving along highways, it's hard to miss those overhead LED signs displaying traffic safety messages. As a writer, it's likely you appreciate the imaginative spin they sometimes put on them.

Some messages are strictly business, warning of a lane closing or a road crew ahead. But sometimes they make an effort to be memorable. Here are a few slogans you may have seen:

ALERT TODAY - ALIVE TOMORROW
FAST DRIVE COULD BE LAST DRIVE
BOOZE IT AND LOSE IT
DRIVING FASTER CAN CAUSE DISASTER
BETTER TO BE MISTER LATE THAN LATE MISTER

I often try to imagine the person who's writing these. If they work for the Department of Transportation, it's probably their most creative moment of the day.

Here's a message that I actually saw yesterday while driving along I-40 in Memphis:

AVOID A WRECK - DON'T RUBBERNECK

I kept an eye out for the accident it might be referring to, but saw none and wrote it off as a generic admonishment. Ironically, driving past the same stretch of highway three hours later, there was indeed an accident near that very spot. Apparently, Confucius was doing the signs yesterday. Then again, on I-40 it was bound to come true sooner or later.

But it got me thinking about the sign again and the fact that people do have a tendency to rubberneck. As drivers inched their way past the tow trucks, they seemed to pay less attention to the policemen directing traffic than they did the state of the cars involved and whether any victims could be seen. (Don't worry, it wasn't that bad of an accident.)

People inherently want to know who, what, when, where, how, and why, even when it's really none of our business. We turn on the news at night to see what happened to people we don't know in places we've never been to.

Don Henley's '80s hit "Dirty Laundry" included a line that has always stuck with me: "It's interesting when people die." Dark as that sentiment seems, it's the truth, and maybe it has something to do with our own underlying sense of mortality, visiting it from a distance and coming out alive. That would be a question for our psychologist author friends, and you know who you are.

All of this is terrific news for writers. Since people are curious by nature, they are always in search of a good story, making them willing to invest the time it takes to read about the imaginary characters you've cooked up for them. As we write, it's a good practice to think about these rubbernecking readers and what kind of details they are hoping to get out of the experience.

Meanwhile, drive safely, and let's flash our lights in honor of the writer who hatched up this one:

DONATE BLOOD, BUT NOT ON ROADS

Chapter 6
PACING

"Pacing has become more important than ever, largely because of other media. I've always tried to start my stories out with a bang, something that will hook their attention."

Will Hobbs

FORTUNATELY/UNFORTUNATELY

It's been around for a few years, so perhaps you've heard of a little game called "Fortunately/Unfortunately". This verbal amusement requires nothing more than people to play it. You simply take turns making up a story, alternating sentences with the first words "fortunately" and "unfortunately". Here's an example:

"Fortunately, I won a trip to Paris."
"Unfortunately, I don't know a word of French."
"Fortunately, I have a translation app on my phone."
"Unfortunately, I had a flat tire as I was leaving for the airport."
"Fortunately, AAA changed it and I made it just in time."
"Unfortunately, I forgot my ticket."

...and so on.

It's a creative way to fill time, like on a long car ride. It's also good exercise for both sides of the brain, since logic and imagination must work together in order to keep the game going.

But this runaway train of thought concept has even greater possibilities for a writer. Isn't "fortunately/unfortunately" the pattern followed by the classic stories? For example:

The Wizard of Oz (skipping ahead to the fun parts):

Fortunately, a good witch gives Dorothy magic shoes to protect her.
Unfortunately, a wicked witch wants the magic shoes.
Fortunately, the Wizard of Oz can help Dorothy return home.
Unfortunately, it's a long walk to get to the wizard.
Fortunately, there's a yellow brick road to guide her.
Unfortunately, she gets lost at a crossroad.
Fortunately, she meets a scarecrow who knows the way.
Unfortunately, he doesn't have a brain.

...and so on.

Following this pattern of "I have good news and bad news," the audience enjoys a roller coaster of ups and downs to keep things interesting. And, it's helpful if the writer knows how it's all going to end so that each scene furthers the plot in the proper direction.

It's not uncommon for a writer to insert several "unfortunatelys" between each "fortunately". Like Sisyphus forever trying to roll a boulder up a hill, problem may pile upon problem before a reprieve temporarily breaks the tension. This is especially common in a dark tale or an action drama.

And the "unfortunately" doesn't always have to be the direct antithesis to what comes before. It can be something completely unpredictable that turns everything on a dime. Who would have anticipated that a cyclone would interfere with Dorothy's running away from home? Any roadblock to the overall goal can do the trick.

Just as when playing the game itself, allow your imagination to run free and spin numerous fortunately/unfortunately scenarios, spontaneously and without overthinking. Let the muse do the work, and in no time at all you could have a working outline for your novel.

WHAT ARE YOUR HEADLINES?

Check any day's news feed and it will typically cover the gamut from celebrity fluff to a world on the brink. As I write these words, for example, one of today's headlines finds it worth reporting that someone from a reality show has had a baby. In other news, North Korea is testing weapons of mass destruction.

There you have one news story with no impact on the average person's life, alongside a news story with considerably greater potential. Which of these stories, if you were to put them in your novel, would keep your reader up at night turning pages?

Fact is, either one is fair game, since both comedy and drama can easily exploit the challenges of something as conventional as parenthood, while the threat of nuclear war is a spy thriller staple. Perhaps even better, combine them: if the undercover agent's identity gets in the wrong hands just as his wife or daughter has given birth, does that not raise the stakes for the hero?

The point is, every life event, however big or small, can have a role in a story if it furthers the plot or adds a layer of interest. Like reporters always looking for a scoop, storytellers need look no further than the daily events around us to find plausible plot points and twists.

As you look back over your own life, there are certain episodes that stand out in your mind more than others. These headlines of your life are step one if you're writing a memoir, but any one of them makes you uniquely qualified to fictionalize it as an event in your novel. You had to live through it; why not capitalize on it?

It's good to think of the significant events in your novel as if they were headlines, and to make each one newsworthy. Some may be a personal crisis just for the hero while others may be the basis for widespread panic. Give your characters captivating headlines to live out, and your audience will stick around to read all about it.

CONSTANT CONFLICT

I love boot camp.

Mind you, I'm a peace-loving guy with pacifist leanings, but I've always been riveted by scenes involving new recruits meeting their merciless drill sergeant and being taken through the rigors of basic training.

Hollywood loves war movies. Conflict is perhaps never portrayed bigger and bolder than in a battle scene. But the face-to-face tension of an underdog trying to keep it together under dire conditions is human drama we can all relate to.

A workplace with a tyrant boss, a classroom with an unreasonable teacher, in-laws who can't be pleased, even domestic quarrels, are ready sources of inherent tension that can escalate our protagonist's real problems. Such challenges come in infinite varieties, but if they are resolved as part of a happy ending, these subplots are typically addressed in one of two ways:

1. The troublemaker gets their comeuppance

The conniving co-worker is exposed, the miserly uncle gets arrested for embezzlement, the contentious neighbor breaks a leg falling off a ladder, and the hero is right there to enjoy it.

2. The troublemaker turns out to be an ally

The overzealous drill sergeant eventually reveals his human side. When the hero rises to the challenge and their strained relationship takes on a hint of mutual respect, it becomes clear that everything the sergeant put him through was for his own good. That moment delivers a satisfying character arc for both of them.

Anyone or anything that stands in the way of our hero's success makes for good conflict along the way. The everyday scenarios that we inflict on our hero can cause hardship right along with the main crisis involving the actual antagonist.

Page-turning prose relies on the story's ability to keep the problems coming. Providing that steady supply of friction in your fiction can ensure that your reader doesn't go AWOL.

GIVING THEM PAUSE

An effective story is a roller coaster ride. It takes readers through a series of twists and turns, saving the biggest thrill for last. And, gravity being what it is, what goes up must come down. It's not one continuous fast drop. Indeed, the slow, steep inclines of anticipation can provide some of the biggest excitement.

Those ups and downs give a story its rhythm, much like breathing. The action builds, then it lets up a bit, then builds again. A problem arises and the hero somewhat settles the matter just in time for more trouble to come.

A story that builds and builds and never gives the reader a chance to catch their breath can be exhausting. If the heart-pounding opening sequence of *Raiders of the Lost Ark* had lasted for two hours without a break, brains would have melted.

An actual example of this (well, not the brain-melting part) is 2005's *King Kong* with Jack Black. Fun movie with interesting variations on an old theme, but once they get to the jungle it's a nonstop series of action sequences. The long prehistoric battles are exciting at first, but about the third or fourth one in, they lose their impact and even become tiresome because there isn't a quiet moment in-between to remind us how amazing these scenes are.

We know that each scene in our story must further the plot, but we can accomplish this in a variety of ways besides perpetual motion. Sometimes the scene will be less about action and more about reaction; the result of what big thing just took place. The bigger the thing, the more the audience will appreciate an opportunity to consider its implications. Give them time to sort out the possibilities for themselves and you have a captive, involved audience.

After a scene with a car crash, the quietude of the patient

lying in a hospital bed isn't just a natural aftermath, but a welcome opportunity to take a cleansing breath and ponder what the new developments will mean.

Sometimes the pause itself provides the drama. In *Hope Springs* with Meryl Streep and Tommy Lee Jones, a particularly important scene is followed by the lengthy closeup shot of a door, which, at that point, seems to last for an eternity. As we look at the door we are filled with questions: 1) which door is this? 2) which of the two people will walk through it? 3) are they coming or going? 4) will the door even open? and 5) what are the ramifications of each of these scenarios? It really is a brilliant and powerful silent story beat in its own right.

As a classic soft drink campaign once reminded us, it's the pause that refreshes. Give your reader a chance to catch their breath before and after your roller coaster's big loops so they'll stand in line to ride some more.

SILENCE IS GOLDEN

A particularly good example of the power of the pause is seen in 2011's *The Descendants* with George Clooney. Frequently, in the midst of a storyline filled with twists and turns, director Alexander Payne follows each big revelation with lingering shots of Hawaiian scenery. Not only does it give the audience time to absorb the latest repercussion, it offers an ironic contrast of beauty in the midst of tragedy. The combination allows for rich moments of deep thought.

For a movie or TV show, such timing is easily dictated in the editing booth. But when writing fiction, how are we to control the timing of our story so the audience feels that same moment of silence? Inserting a pause into a novel can be as simple as closing a scene or a chapter at the moment of impact:

> "I don't think she'll be coming in today."
> "Why not?"
> "She's dead."

If more dialogue or exposition is necessary before ending the scene, another technique is to stop the dialogue momentarily and allow the characters some reaction time:

"I don't think she'll be coming in today."
"Why not?"
"She's dead."
The blood drained from Larry's face, and he thought he might pass out. He fumbled behind him for a chair and slid into it.
"She never signed the papers, did she?"

If dialogue simply barrels along without acknowledging the shock of the moment, the reader is equally unlikely to perceive its impact. By providing a moment of silence, they are given an unspoken opportunity to contemplate the revelation.

Heavy-handed though they can be, soap operas know the value of zooming in on the stunned faces of the characters after any big announcement, giving the audience ample time for implications to sink in before cutting away to a commercial. We can take a cue from these masters of melodrama to effectively create pregnant pauses of our own.

THE COVENANT OF THE ARC

For many writers, the character arc is a vague concept which can feel like an imposition. When we already have an interesting plot that's fun to write, why must we burden ourselves with the laborious task of transforming our protagonist into a new and better person?

First of all, because the reader wants it. Secondly, it's not as difficult or nebulous as it sounds.

The plot may be the driving force behind the story, but as good as it may be, that only covers the external. It is through the *internal* struggle of the hero that the reader will invest themselves and feel the real heart of the story.

Perhaps you've noticed how many famous tales feature an orphan. Before the plot even develops, the protagonist is a sympathetic character lacking the stability of a true home. An Oliver Twist will experience his emotional arc by looking for love in all the wrong places but ending up finding a family. A Harry Potter will go from being a neglected child to claiming his rightful place in the world.

Similarly, in many classic Westerns as well as modern-day action flicks, the hero's family dies early on. These lost souls who have had life as they know it taken away from them can experience their arc in a variety of ways: revenge, restitution, etc. A Jason Bourne, who loses both his memory and his identity, can regain his footing by discovering who he really is.

How many romances feature a selfish, stuck-up protagonist who ultimately finds the meaning of love and is transformed into happily-ever-after material? Yes, it's a cliché, but the audience eats it up when the character recognizes that they were their own worst enemy.

The Farrelly Brothers' comedy *Shallow Hal* stars Jack Black as a man who judges everyone by their looks. When Tony Robbins hypnotizes Hal and causes him to see people for who they really are, he finds true love with someone he would have totally ignored. Something as simple as a lesson learned is a sturdy arc.

When writing a book series, only minor protagonist arcs are advised, because the audience wants the hero to stay comfortably familiar from book to book. Even when the womanizing James Bond got married at one point, his wife was out of the picture before the next book.

In literature you will see no lack of Scrooges who discover there is more to life than money, and adventurers who leave the safety of their world to go find themselves only to realize that there's no place like home.

And here's a tip: arcs aren't just for the main character. A story wins extra points for depth when secondary characters get in on the action. Someone who is an antagonist early on could well become an advocate for the hero when we least expect it. This can be doubly satisfying because they not only help save the day for the protagonist, but also demonstrate a change of heart themselves.

Each of us experience arcs of many kinds on a regular basis. In the course of a lifetime, we couldn't count them all. Luckily, we only have to build one arc for our hero to give him or her (and the reader) the emotional anchor they're hoping for.

GOING FULL CIRCLE

It seems like just yesterday we'd be flipping the pages of the latest *Archie* or *Batman* comic book and would come across this headline:

"Tired of being picked on? Nobody picks on an ATLAS MAN!"

The cartoon panels accompanying this full-page ad showed a beach bully kicking sand at a skinny fellow (named Mac) and his girl. After confronting and being threatened by the muscle-bound brute, Mac vows to get even some day. In the next panel, he signs up for Charles Atlas' bodybuilding course, and in the end he becomes the hero of the beach.

The word balloons changed over the years, I noticed, so sometimes Mac's girl was sympathetic as he pitifully vowed revenge. Other times she said something demeaning like, "Oh, don't let it *bother* you, little boy." Originally, the cartoon showed the aftermath of a now-powerful Mac knocking the beach bully out. Over time, the advertisement eliminated that panel, probably because it promoted violence. Or maybe Mac punched out his verbally abusive girlfriend off-screen.

The point is, in the unabridged version of this miniature morality tale, we are given a definitive "before" and "after". Before, Mac is picked on by a bully. After, the underdog becomes top dog.

This classic Atlas ad is a simple but effective example of the full circle readers want in their stories. There has to be a situation that needs resolving, and by the end of the story that situation must be resolved. Without either, there is no sense of accomplishment.

This return to the "ordinary world" will clarify the results of what has taken place and show how things—and hopefully the hero—have changed. The hero doesn't physically have to return to their hometown with a parade waiting for them. Sometimes the hero in fact cannot go back to their world, but an early vulnerability that is now a strength is easy to convey.

If the character arc is apparent enough, it may not even be necessary to change a thing. A mere reminder of how things used to be could be sufficient. Perhaps the hero was swimming at the beginning of the story. Toward the end of the story, the hero is swimming again. Same activity, but this time *we* know they possess a contentment they didn't have the first time.

Life itself affords us very few clear-cut befores and afters, so we find fulfillment in those we experience with our fictional friends. Letting readers go full circle via the bookends of an obvious before and after is an easy and effective way to bulk up a skinny story.

ENDING IS BETTER THAN PENDING

Over lunch some years ago, I was taken aback when a friend declared that he usually reads the last page of a book before deciding whether to read the whole thing. It seemed like a highly irregular approach to me. Since then, however, other acquaintances have echoed that they too engage in this inhuman practice.

"Why would you want to read the book after you know how it ends?" I ask. The answer may vary, but it invariably involves some defense that it doesn't diminish their enjoyment. They argue something about a good story standing up to repeat visits, like a favorite movie. At that point the conversation turns into a discussion of our favorite movies, and we never get back to the original subject.

If some booklovers like to start at the finish line, more power to them. In fact, starting at the end isn't just a favored trait of the odd reader, it is also a winning strategy of many writers.

Mystery authors in particular must possess a sense of whodunit and howtheydunit long before the climactic chapters. How else can clues and red herrings be strategically planted along the way?

Truth is, foreknowledge of the finale isn't just for mystery writers. No matter the genre, there are multiple benefits to be had, even for pantsers devoted to writing freeform.

Having decided on the ending allows us to prepare for the big finish in ways that will enhance it. Imagine an ending where the newlywed heroes are driving off into the sunset in a sparkling new Lamborghini. A pleasant enough ending. But it can add an extra layer of emotional satisfaction if, earlier in the story, that very vehicle was out of reach to them in a showroom.

The opportunity to foreshadow is another plus to knowing where you're going. If the young man's future father-in-law is the CEO of a boat manufacturing company, how much irony would there be if we know that the young man's own dad had taken him fishing every weekend?

Perhaps the biggest benefit to having the ending already mapped out is that it will keep you from wasting time writing nonessential scenes that don't push the plot in the right direction. Your first draft will have more focus and there'll be less to leave on the cutting room floor.

Whether we're working toward a bitter end or a happily-ever-after, a well-planned finish from the start can become a story's be-all and end-all.

EPILOGUE, THE UNDERDOG

You may have noticed a storytelling trick that is used repeatedly, especially in action movies. After the climactic face-to-face battle between the hero and the antagonist comes to a close, the dust settles on a lingering faraway shot, the music ends, and the screen fades to black. You *know* from experience that there's one more scene to come. But the black lasts longer than you would expect . . . long enough to make you wonder if indeed it is the end and the credits are about to roll.

Then, one more final scene does appear, and you think, "Ah, they got me again." But, as always, you're glad to see it.

Whether we're kept in suspense waiting for it or not, the epilogue is reassuring in its familiarity, and a chance to give the audience time to recover from a big finish before they rise from their seats and head to the car. More importantly, from a storytelling standpoint, it's their chance to assess everything they've just experienced and learn what it means to the characters and the world they live in.

Getting fancy, the epilogue is known in some circles as the *denouement*, meaning "the final resolution of the intricacies of a plot." It's all about cause and effect. When something happens, we are inherently curious to know the result.

The epilogue is exactly where you'll see the other end of the character arc our hero has been through. With that in mind, you're doing yourself a favor if you anticipate early on what an ideal epilogue for your story would be, allowing you to put the means in place as you write everything that precedes.

Some authors dismiss the epilogue as being too cliché. However, bringing a story to an abrupt ending without providing the aftermath is like taking the reader on a journey and not giving them a ride back.

So really, the "big finish" isn't the finish at all. That final confrontation where the hero overcomes the enemy is only a momentary thrill. The real takeaway is what it means once it has taken place.

As *Dune* author Frank Herbert said, "There is no real ending. It's just the place where you stop the story." Providing a closer that leaves readers with a satisfying sense of the aftermath is the secret to making ends meet.

MAKING ENDS MEET

The great philosopher Taylor Swift once said, "I love the ending of a movie where two people end up together. Preferably if there's rain and an airport or running or a confession of love." I think we may have seen that movie.

Of course, what we don't see is what comes after the proposal. We usually don't see the happy couple getting blood tests, dealing with paperwork at the registrar's office, trying to lose weight for the wedding, or arguing a year later because someone didn't take out the trash.

"If you want a happy ending," said Orson Welles, that depends, of course, on where you stop your story." Indeed, most stories end at the point where there is a happy ending, a resolve, or a sense of hope. Ever since man began telling stories, *beginning/middle/end* has been the gold standard.

But in the early days of film, movie makers realized audiences would keep coming back week after week if they were given a story that has no ending. Thus were born short features like *Flash Gordon, Superman, The Perils of Pauline,* and other cliffhangers starring recurring good guys, bad guys, and damsels in distress, some with heroes literally hanging from cliffs until the next installment.

That same serialized approach became a staple of radio once it came along. Even the comedy Amos & Andy had its roots as a fractured drama, complete with a somber opening theme. Within a couple of decades, soap operas dominated TV. Romance and drama are a natural mix for a storyline that has no ending. No sooner is one problem solved when three more come along.

Today, the "continuing saga" concept is more popular than ever. It's all over television and streaming video, from Game of Thrones to Peaky Blinders. Miss one episode and you'll miss some event so pivotal that you'll be scratching your head down the road.

But these are not simply long sagas with no end. Each episode includes its own situation to be dealt with, and while we are still baited with a cliffhanger, we receive some measure of conclusion to the drama du jour. Otherwise it would get frustrating to invest repeatedly in something that never pays off because the story is forever stuck in the middle.

We have an inherent craving for resolve. Like the tales we tell, our lives contain constant ups and downs, but when we succeed, the world doesn't stop to acknowledge each victory with "THE END". We love a hero we can identify with and through whom we feel the elusive sense of closure.

If we've written solid characters, their lives could continue beyond the ending of our story. Choosing the most satisfying place to close the epilogue is how we give readers what they desire. They are thankful for happy endings, because real life tends to be one big cliffhanger.

SECTION III

THE CAST OF CHARACTERS

Chapter 7
THE HERO

"Heroes are made by the path they choose, not the powers they are graced with."

Brodi Ashton

WHO'S ON FIRST?

At the beginning of every story, the audience is ready to meet the new set of characters you've dreamed up for them. One of the challenges in writing that opening scene can be deciding which of your characters to introduce first.

In its original Greek, the word *protagonist* means "first in importance". While this person will be the central figure of the story, we don't always need to make them the first to appear. There will be times when it's advantageous to wait and bring them in later.

Taking a cue from stage plays, especially musicals, the star of the show is often saved until the end of the big opening number. In *West Side Story*, both street gangs establish their roughhouse hatred for one another in song and dance long before we ever meet Tony or Maria. In many cases, this is to allow a Broadway star to make their own magnificent entrance. But this approach can also allow for a little discussion about the hero before they arrive on the scene, affording advance information about their importance.

Then again, in *The Addams Family* stage musical, the entire ensemble (complete with stars Nathan Lane and Bebe Neuwirth) appeared onstage from the get-go. These familiar characters needed no introduction, and the sum of the whole had much greater initial impact than if they had been introduced individually.

And there's *The Sound of Music*, which begins with the heroine joyfully spinning and singing solo on a hilltop. We learn up front how much both music and her surroundings mean to her before anything else takes place.

One of the most inventive character introductions I've ever read started with opening paragraphs describing a fellow walking through a college campus. It spoke of him appreciating seasonal decorations and other pleasant details, and at one point he stopped along the way to help someone. Without a word of dialogue, and without knowing much of anything about this fellow, we already identified with him and liked him.

But then, when this fellow arrived at his destination, which turned out to be hiding behind the girls' locker room, the tide began to turn in a very uncomfortable way. The author had managed to make the reader bond unwittingly with the villain of the story. Disquieting, and brilliant.

In a murder mystery or crime drama, the bad guy will often appear before the hero does, if only in shadow. By the time Perry Mason is called in, the trouble has already begun and he's playing the hero from his very first scene. It's unlikely we'll see him lounging at his desk with his feet up waiting for something to happen, because it already has. This sequence is typical in a series, where we are already familiar with the lead character who will carry the adventure.

Who the audience should be introduced to first can sometimes be determined by their role in the story. Will everything revolve around their wants and needs, with a huge character arc ahead? Or are they more a participant in a bigger theme (like class struggle, as in *Romeo and Juliet*)? That conflict on a larger scale may be the thing to establish first.

Whether you place your protagonist in the first paragraph or save them for a grand entrance, the star of your story deserves a proper introduction via fortuitous timing.

PUTTING THE PRO IN PROTAGONIST

Writers often use the words "protagonist" and "hero" interchangeably, and for good reason. If we look at the actual definitions, we can see why:

Protagonist: The leading character in a drama, movie, novel, or other fictional text.

Hero: A person who is admired for their courage or noble qualities.

When we create the lead character in our story, we want it to be someone the audience likes, respects, and cares about. We do that best by giving the protagonist heroic qualities.

Not to say that our lead needs to leap tall buildings in a single bound, nor do they even need to leave the house. They need only possess one or more character traits our audience will value. We admire a character who's witty, smart, talented, or humane—basically the same qualities we want in.

We've all observed main characters who were none of these things. And it's likely we never finished those books and films once we realized the protagonist was someone we simply didn't find likable or relatable, someone we didn't care to spend the next two hours or three hundred pages with.

One of the few movies I've ever walked out on was a 1990s flick by a well-known director in which the protagonist had multiple personalities. The subject matter looked interesting enough, but it only took twenty minutes of this guy going back and forth between annoying personas possessing no redeeming qualities among them, for me to decide to sneak into a showing of *3 Ninjas* instead. Had the protagonist done anything to make someone care about what happened to him, I might have stuck around. But in this case, he wasn't a hero, but merely the central figure of the story.

Save the Cat!, Blake Snyder and Jessica Brody's outstanding book series on story creation, gets its very title from the importance of having your main character do something "nice" early on so that the audience will bond with him/her. The hero will do a good deed or exhibit some moment of quality behavior that causes the audience to identify with them.

In *Where the Crawdads Sing*, the heroine—a suspected murderess—literally befriends a cat while she in the county jail.

"Saving the cat" symbolically is a scene from *Sea of Love* in which a tough cop (Al Pacino) has organized a sting operation disguised as a Major League Baseball breakfast. After containing a ballroom full of offenders with outstanding warrants, he steps outside to find one of his intended victims arriving late with his young son, excited about meeting their baseball hero. Instead of ushering him inside where handcuffs await, Pacino takes the child into consideration. He tells that dad there's no more room and lets them leave. "Catch you later," he says.

Saving the cat (delivering the "care package", as James Scott Bell calls it) is something we can accomplish even for an antihero. In fact, many a protagonist starts out as a self-consumed, erroneous figure, which makes their character arc that much more dramatic when they are reformed. Whoever the hero is, a well-told story will establish early on that this person deserves a good outcome.

By the same token, we want them to have flaws. Perfect protagonists are boring. Make sure your hero has vulnerabilities everyone can identify with; weaknesses than can take him/her down. Kryptonite only goes so far as a general threat, but human conflict is the stuff of legend in fiction.

Any time a reader picks up your book, they're hoping for a story that will envelope them. When you give them a relatable protagonist they can share an adventure with, and ultimately prevail with, the real hero is you.

THERE OUGHTA BE A FLAW

In virtually every story we write, it's a given that we will give our hero challenges to face. Those obstacles we put in his/her path are likely to be external in nature, delivered by either circumstances or an antagonist. But we can increase the drama further by slipping in some internal struggles for our hero too.

Besides making our protagonist more lifelike, a character flaw has the power to add the fascinating element of *irony*. A hero who becomes the guardian of his brother's kids will have a worse time of it if he had vowed never to have children. An eyewitness in a murder trial will find it harder to testify if he was somewhere he wasn't supposed to be.

The "inner demon" doesn't have to be anything illegal, immoral, or fattening. It can be a guilty conscience, an ethical dilemma, the tug of war between the angel on one shoulder and the devil on the other. Anything that creates personal turmoil is material for mayhem.

It can feel against the grain to make our hero imperfect, especially if we write in first person, because our own voice is inherently caught up in there on a conscious or unconscious level. If it helps to distance you from your character, seek out a trait you don't possess.

Need some ideas? The Seven Deadly Sins could be a source of inspiration. If you can remember all seven and don't have to look them up, more power to you. I can usually only remember the ones I've gotten good at.

If you find it difficult to give your beloved hero a flaw, consider a vulnerability instead. What's the difference? One would consider chronic grouchiness a flaw, whereas a fear of heights amounts to a vulnerability. Simply put, a flaw is something we can change; a vulnerability is something we cannot. It isn't Indiana Jones' fault that he's afraid of snakes. (Although I suppose he could get therapy for that.)

Depending on what you're going for, a vulnerability can elicit sympathy more than a flaw. At the same time, a flaw is a handy idiosyncrasy you can work into your character arc.

The most unflawed character in all of fiction would probably have to be Superman. Here's a guy who possesses superhuman powers and uses them for the public good. Yet he is vulnerable to kryptonite, much less the designs of a femme fatale who steals his invincible heart. If Superman didn't possess qualities that could weaken him, he would be as plastic as the toys made in his image.

Whether our protagonist is a "hero" in the most literal sense of the word, or an underdog who must rise from the ashes, we give our story layers by including an Achilles heel above and beyond the main conflict. The reader may not have personal experience with a tsunami or a kidnapping, but everyone knows what it's like to be human.

YOUR HERO NEEDS HANGUPS

We've talked a lot about giving our characters goals, then putting obstacles in their path so they have difficulty achieving them. We can double that drama by making their obstacles ones that not only impede their progress, but ones which they already possess a deep-seated fear of.

Consider Jack Nicholson's character in the film *As Good As It Gets*. His obsessive-compulsive disorder is constantly put to the test for him to even have a shot at getting the girl. The internal roadblock provides a means for conflict at every turn.

Phobias in fiction are worth their weight in gold. Indiana Jones had a problem with snakes, and part of the fun of *Raiders* was seeing how he reacted to a roomful of asps.

We identify with a hero who has hangups, since we tend to have a few of our own. A warrior without worries is unrelatable. It would be hard to identify with Superman if his invincible body didn't have that soft spot for Lois Lane.

For all its faults, reality TV is artfully adept at exploiting contestants' fears. From *Fear Factor* (eating bugs) to *Bear Gryllis' Running Wild* (rock climbing and eating bugs), we're facing our own fears alongside the players, wondering how far we would be willing to go if $5000 was dangled in front of us. Similarly, we are drawn into a story in which the protagonist is challenged on a deeply personal level. The specific quest may not be one we ever have to face, but then again, something inside us does like to feel prepared.

Fears we can all relate to include:

Fear of failure
Loss of freedom
Loss of a job
Unrequited love
The unknown

The biggest fear of all, of course, is death. Physical danger of any kind is an intrinsic phobia everyone knows. But even something as simple as disappointment can be a worthwhile challenge to our hero, giving us a very wide berth within which to endanger their destiny.

"We have met the enemy and he is us," Pogo once said. We can up the ante of antagonism by giving our protagonist a good internal struggle to deal with on top of their outside enemies and obstacles.

Inner demons add an easy and especially effective layer of conflict since our internal fears are among the hardest to conquer. Don't be afraid to use them.

THE HAUNTED HERO

A good protagonist has issues. No matter how strong and resilient they may be, a solid hero comes with baggage.

In real life, emotional baggage can be painful to explore and is often ignored. For the storyteller, however, it's a favorite device to give the hero depth. The basic plot will throw challenges their way, but it's the inner conflict they themselves bring to the story that can create some of the most intriguing and relatable tension.

For example, in many famous stories, the hero blames themself for a family member's death. If we are aware of the incident, it barely needs elaboration. Even if nothing is said of it, we understand innately what the hero's thought process must be when reminders and other challenges present themselves.

The sort of things that haunt our hero can involve any brand of turmoil: death, guilt, abandonment, shame, rejection, you name it. The cause of their self-torture may take place within the action of the story itself, or it may be expressed in a reveal after much of the story has taken place.

The latter method is a handy way to pique the reader's curiosity if they are given clues along the way suggesting there is more to the hero than meets the eye. Ideally, it will relate in some way to the plot itself so that they can gain some victory over it as part of their ultimate arc.

Baggage is not only good for the protagonist; it makes for a more fascinating antagonist as well. Most of us know that Batman wouldn't have become a caped crusader had it not been for a tragedy in his youth. But let's not forget that Joker also has a troubled past that he considers to be a valid excuse for his mayhem.

Does their baggage always have to be bad? Not necessarily. Writer Hope Alcocer shares this brilliant explanation: "Behind every dancer there's someone that broke her, a song that moved her, a moment that inspired her, and a dance floor that healed her." The emotional weight that we lug around makes us who we are for all of life's ups and downs.

Before our heroes embark on whatever quest we send them on, the trip is certain to be more interesting if we remember to pack some believable baggage for their hero's journey.

WHEN BAD THINGS HAPPEN TO GOOD PROTAGONISTS

When readers are seeking to be entertained, it's all about things going badly for the hero. With a fictional character as our proxy, we can pretend we, too, are facing our fears and prevailing, just as he/she hopefully will.

No one seeks hardship upon themselves, and when given the choice we choose the lesser of two evils. Our hero has the same instinct for self-preservation, so they will try to avoid trouble at all cost. Which is why problems often will be thrust upon them by someone with an opposing agenda.

"Good people do not need laws to tell them to act responsibly," said Plato, "while bad people will find a way around the laws." This great forefather of fiction knew that characters with a propensity for doing bad are good at creating conflict for a sympathetic hero.

In instances when trouble strikes as a result of an outside force, our innocent victim is considered a *passive* protagonist.

On the other hand—just as in real life—trouble can be self-inflicted, caused by the hero's own carelessness, bad judgment, stubbornness, or other misstep. This *active* protagonist can attract adversity, even if it's due to good intentions gone wrong. He or she will set out to accomplish something, only to have it go awry.

In general, writers are told to avoid the passive protagonist because readers don't invest themselves as readily in a hero to whom things merely happen. They wish to identify with someone who wants something and is intent on getting it.

The ideal plot, it would seem, will star an active protagonist capable of causing his own calamity (the archetypical flawed hero), only to be further thwarted by an equally active antagonist who brings even more tribulation to the table. Our poor imperfect protagonist can't get a break. They have an enemy but can also be their own worst enemy.

The goal is to pile on however much misfortune it takes to convince the reader that all is lost; that there's no possible way the hero is going to come out on top. They will, of course. But it's all the roadblocks threatening that victory which keep the reader turning the page, since trouble—no matter who's causing it—is just plain interesting.

ISN'T IT IRONIC

When George Bailey decides to drown himself in *It's a Wonderful Life*, he ends up saving someone else from drowning instead. Over the course of the story, George realizes his life isn't worthless after all, but rather has had positive impact on everyone around him. Irony such as this adds a touch of magic to fiction; a poetic twist of fate that makes it bigger than life.

In reality, life itself is full of ironies, so we identify with this fictional device. From Greek tragedies forward, storytellers have sought to heighten the drama by pitting characters and situations against themselves.

There's enough irony in the movie *Titanic* to sink a ship. The rich girl doesn't want her rich suitor; she loves the poor immigrant boy. Many on board were looking to start a new life, only to have no future at all. There were too few lifeboats available because a maritime disaster like this was never going to happen, much less on the maiden voyage.

In *The Wizard of Oz*, everyone puts their hope in a wizard who isn't a wizard at all. Dorothy runs away from home, then wants to return almost immediately. Her traveling companions long for a brain, a heart, and courage, when it turns out they had them all along.

More recently, *The Fault in Our Stars* features a character who likes to keep a cigarette in his mouth but never lights up, in metaphorical defiance against the cancer stick.

There is irony in a flawed protagonist. Even superheroes and crimefighters will have at least one serious Achilles heel. To makes matters worse for costumed crusaders from Spiderman to Zorro, they can't reveal their secret identity to the people they love most, and often get blamed for something they didn't do.

Contrast is a particularly popular form of irony. His messy roommate exasperates neatnik Felix Unger in Neil Simon's *The Odd Couple*. Similarly, Sesame Street's Bert and Ernie were a pint-sized pair of opposites. From *The King and I* to *My Fair Lady* to *Downton Abbey*, there is fascination in seeing different cultures and classes clash.

How many fictional romances start out with the two lovers despising each other? (Besides virtually every one of them?) Of course, we wouldn't be quite as interested if it were love at first sight and remained smooth sailing through the tunnel of love.

Similarity can be just as ironic as contrast. We see it in a child who takes on the negative characteristics of a parent, or a sidekick who comes to the rescue by using a skill the hero had taught them.

The very jokes we tell make us laugh through irony. We are surprised by the punchline because we were expecting something else. Why did the duck cross the road? Because it was the chicken's day off.

Irony comes in many different forms and creates interest instantly. We can give a story more layers and richer complexity with the simple addition of this very easy device. How ironic is that?

GONE BUT NOT FORGOTTEN

A good protagonist is like a good friend. Over time we get attached to them as if they were members of the family. So when writers decide to kill them off, a little piece of us dies with them.

The Grim Reaper has been no stranger to series like *House of Cards, The 100, Game of Thrones* and, like the title implies, *The Walking Dead*. Cop shows and mysteries feature death by default, but when the deceased is a fan favorite, it's a shocking turn of events.

In a memorable conversation with a writer friend, I was mourning the loss of a primary character on one of the few TV dramas I used to follow, *The Blacklist*. After my rant, they in turn bemoaned the impending doom soon to befall a key character on a drama they follow just as avidly. All of this was on the heels of the blockbuster *Batman vs Superman*, in which a beloved character met their demise.

Getting rid of a main character in a film or TV series is sometimes the practical real-world result of a pregnancy, a contract dispute, or some other irreconcilable difference. Fortunately, writers of book series don't get painted into such corners with actors, so literary deaths have a bit more intentionality to them. It seems the more dystopian the setting, the more likely it is that one or more of the good guys won't make it to the last installment.

No matter the medium, extinguishing a popular character is a bold move. More than one author has faced backlash from angry readers afterwards. J.K. Rowling made postmortem apologies almost an annual tradition. As far back as 1893, Sir Arthur Conan Doyle felt the brunt of a perturbed public when he killed off Sherlock Holmes. The outcry was so loud that he soon resurrected the storied sleuth.

If a main character must die, it should further the plot and not be merely for shock value (or publicity). If it provides fodder for subsequent episodes that deal with finding the person's killer, for example, at least they did not die in vain. The bereaved audience will find solace and satisfaction as justice is sought and served.

At the very least, the impact a character death has on the reading or viewing public must be given appropriate consideration. The audience needs time to grieve, so let them attend the funeral, hear the recollections of the deceased's friends and family, and basically say goodbye in their own way.

Since there are innumerable ways to wipe out a protagonist, the pen is indeed mightier than the sword. If you should find yourself with a good reason to try it in your novel, proceed with caution, but be encouraged by those who've gone before you. Obviously some writers are making a killing doing it.

GIVING THEM GRIEF

Many of us are familiar with the Five Stages of Grief, said to be the emotions we have to work through whenever we suffer a loss or other devastating blow. They are:

Denial
Anger
Bargaining
Depression
Acceptance

We don't always experience them in that order, nor are we necessarily visited by all of them. But this psychological observation is an excellent tool we can use to bring our characters to life.

When we give our hero a challenge, we are essentially taking something important away from them. Whether we kill off their loved one, fire them from a job, or give them a crime to solve, we remove the comfort zone they were previously in. It becomes their task to deal with it, and different characters will do it in different ways.

We've all seen heroes who, when initially approached for help, refuse the call to action. If they don't believe in the cause—or in themselves—they deny the need to take up arms. Soon, however, it becomes personal and they have no choice but to act.

During the course of the story, it's satisfying to experience the same character arc as our protagonist. We identify with their anger and frustration when the villain is getting away with murder. We are right there with the hero, looking for solutions in our own mental bargaining table. We can appreciate how the heroine's romantic slump causes her to eat a whole pint of Häagen-Dazs in one sitting.

However, in the last stage—acceptance—we discover a distinct difference between real life and fiction. We're not content for our heroes merely to *accept* the situation as it stands. We insist that they *overcome*.

Peter Protagonist can't merely come to terms with someone stealing his idea and getting rich from it. Peter has to come up with an even better idea and ultimately steal the thunder back from his opponent.

Harriet Heroine cannot just learn to be at peace with college professors who fail her and cause her to drop out. She must rise from the ashes and become a superstar in her field, so she can throw it back in their faces, as publicly and humiliatingly as possible.

When a young Bruce Wayne grows up to be a caped crusader who captures his parent's murderer, that has a nice full circle feel to it. When the career of the tiger lady in *Baby Boom* goes bust after inheriting a child, we cheer all the more when the baby becomes the very reason she conquers the business world. We love poetic justice.

Confronted by trouble, protagonists go the extra mile and turn into conquerors. When it looks like they'll fail, make them prevail. That's why we call them *heroes*.

Chapter 8
THE ADVERSARY

"The more successful the villain, the more successful the picture."

Alfred Hitchcock

WHAT MAKES A GOOD BAD GUY?

Captain Hook. Hannibal Lecter. Darth Vader. The Wicked Witch of the West. Long John Silver. Dracula. What do these, and countless other villains from literature and movies, have in common? Yes, they all talk kinda funny. But more importantly, each one is infinitely more intriguing than the hero of the story.

Nothing against Peter Pan, Luke Skywalker or our little runaway from Kansas, but the truth is, you could rewrite pretty much every one of these classics and put any character in the protagonist's seat and it would still be the antagonist who steals the show.

A memorable villain can take a tale to epic proportions, even if the hero is an everyday Joe, or a boring do-gooder. Did anyone ever really get excited about Dudley Do-Right?

Even if you've never read the book or seen the movie, you can probably tell me more about the whale in Moby Dick than you can the hero of that story. Which would be whom, by the way? Captain Ahab? Ishmael? It hardly matters, because either one is a mere sardine compared to the dramatic power of the great white whale. Readers had to wade through dozens of chapters about the whaling industry when all they really wanted was a good shipwreck.

Despite all his ingenious methods of transportation and wonderful toys, where would Batman really be without bigger-than-life archenemies to go to bat with? Superheroes become superheroes by conquering supervillains. Haven't you found it disappointing when a bad guy in those stories was just a common street thug? Even Dick Tracy was given crooks who at least looked weird.

And it was only half in jest that I brought up villains having odd speech patterns. *Silence of the Lamb's* Hannibal Lecter's meticulously calculated articulation contributed greatly to his manner of menace. One feels he's so high above us on the intelligence scale that he can suck our mind right out of us. The cackling of a witch or the grunts of a monster solidify them as creatures from our nightmares. At the very least, a foreign accent tends to take us out of our own turf and into unfamiliar territory.

Not that every hero pales in comparison to his foes. Indiana Jones's charisma and humor managed to outshine every nemesis. James Bond steals the screen no matter who's trying to shake and stir him. Name just about any detective or mystery series and the writer has taken care to give that hero or heroine enough personality to carry story after story. But a memorable villain only makes it better.

The bottom line is, a good bad guy is good to find. No matter who the star of your story is, give them a villain so unique and bigger than life that when your protagonist conquers them, they will earn that title of hero.

KEEP THE CONFLICT REAL

"The truth is out there," we are told, but lately it seems to get lost in the shuffle. The more technologically advanced we become, the more we find ourselves bombarded with beguiling deception. From clickbait to slanted news, there is artifice around every corner trying to grab our attention.

These practitioners of prevarication may think they're pulling the wool over our eyes, but the good news is, we writers are too smart for them. As creative thinkers ourselves, we can spot a snow job from down the street.

Much like fast food, "reality" TV has a bad reputation thanks to its generally unhealthy menu. A discerning viewer can tell the difference between a credible documentary like *My 600-lb Life* and the sitcomish silliness of *Chrisley Knows Best*. What they all have in common, however, is *conflict*.

I bring all this up to remind us of two things:

1. People *are entertained* by conflict.
2. A savvy audience can smell fakery.

Whether the drama is bonafide or bogus, the lure of any story lies in the conflict it portrays. But the more believable the conflict, the more we allow ourselves to invest in it.

Book and film critics complain when the villain has no motivation nor backstory. Such a story lacks authenticity because even a bad guy has what he *thinks* is a good reason to give the hero a hard time.

By contrast, it's actual human drama with a touch of suspense each time TV's *Catfish* reels in a big one and pits her face-to-face with the victim of her fake identity. It becomes even more relatable when we learn the reason for the ruse, sometimes even evoking a measure of sympathy for the perpetrator.

A work of fiction carries the ring of truth if there is cause behind the conflict. Yes, the bad guy wants to rob a bank. But why? Because he wants money. But WHY? Because his son needs a kidney transplant. *Now* we have motivation, and when the truth is revealed we may even empathize with the troublemaker.

The bottom line is, keep it real and you'll keep your reader committed. Portraying genuine human drama in the conflict you create for your characters will help you avoid writing flat fiction.

THE VALUE OF A VULNERABLE VILLAIN

Without a worthy foe, a hero is just another joe. It isn't hard to come up with an antagonist whose wants are in direct opposition to those of our protagonist. The trick is creating a bad guy to whom the reader can relate, a connection which inherently increases their investment in the story. To see ourselves reflected in a villain can be quite unsettling.

Who could resist the cultured charm of Hannibal Lecter in *The Silence of the Lambs*? Certainly not FBI ingénue Clarice Starling, in spite of—or perhaps because of—his ability to get into her head. But Hannibal wasn't always a cannibal. His propensity for people eating has its roots in a childhood tragedy in which his own sister was someone's snack. While that would ruin most normal appetites, we can appreciate that it could put a side of insanity on the menu.

Speaking of charmers, long before portraying the intimidating Professor Snape in Harry Potter, Alan Rickman made his mark in the movies by playing *Die Hard's* charismatic terrorist Hans Gruber. (Not to be confused with classical composer Heinz Gruber, although there was a certain artful orchestration to his masterminding.)

We may think of the Wicked Witch of the West as little more than the green face of evil. But you'd be a little miffed too if someone dropped a house on your sister.

Captain Hook's beef with Peter Pan goes way back, but wasn't helped by the fact that the very reason he has a hook is because of Peter. Avenging an injustice, again, can be a powerful motivator.

A pivotal character in *The Fault in Our Stars* seems at first to have no redeeming qualities until the cause of his unsociable behavior is revealed.

A look at most of the classic movie monsters—presumably the most heinous of the horde—reveals a deep-seated humanity, often that of a misunderstood or tortured soul. From the Wolfman to the Frankenstein creation that started it all, most were innocent recipients of their lot in life. Quasimodo and The Phantom of the Opera are at their core pathetic figures deformed by life and a lack of love.

We do well whenever we can cast a villain who is more than

a cardboard cutout of crime. The more relatable he is, the more we sympathize with him, and the more real he becomes.

Basically, we love a villain who has a heart. As long as it's not someone else's.

WHO IS YOUR CONTAGONIST?

Every good story that has conflict (and every good story does have conflict!) includes at least one hero and at least one villain. As savvy storytellers, we look for and easily spot the protagonist and the antagonist.

Protagonist: Harry Potter
Antagonist: Lord Voldemort

Protagonist: Dorothy
Antagonist: The Wicked Witch of the West

Protagonist: Batman
Antagonists: The Joker, The Penguin, Catwoman, countless others

Through experience, we've come to expect that these two archetypes won't come in full head-to-head combat with each other until the final confrontation. The story has to build up to that exciting climax by first leading the hero through a series of challenges. And that's where the *contagonist* comes in.

So who is the *con*tagonist? First, let's affirm that the *pro*tagonist is "for" something (like achieving the main goal) and that the *ant*agonist is "against" it. The *con*tagonist plays a role that is "contrary" to the hero's pursuit. That is, standing in the way of it, or being a distraction from it, though not necessarily with the adversarial intent of an enemy.

For example, Professor Snape could be considered a contagonist for Harry Potter. He's not the villain of the story, but he provides tension and conflict along the way.

You could even look at the wizard of Oz himself as something of a contagonist, because he impedes Dorothy's quest to go home by first giving her a dangerous assignment.

The Silence of the Lambs' Hannibal Lecter is both a collaborator and a complication for Detective Starling. In a buddy comedy like *Dumb and Dumber*, the heroes are often each other's biggest hurdle.

As in the above examples, the line can be blurred between contagonist and ally or any other archetype. That alone can add an extra layer of depth to the story. The contagonist can likewise be an ally of the antagonist, as in the case of a henchman, or perhaps someone in competition with the adversary.

As you might suspect, the contagonist doesn't have to be human. Just as the main antagonist can be an asteroid hurtling toward Earth or a drought that threatens the farm, any person, thing or circumstance that stands between the hero and the achievement of his/her goal can be considered a contagonist.

A winter storm that keeps someone from getting home in time to stop a wedding. A job change. A lost wallet. A flat tire. A surprise visitor. Any of these can throw a curve ball into the mix. None intend to thwart the hero, but they do the trick. *The Out of Towners (1970)* and *Planes, Trains and Automobiles* (1987) are packed with examples of non-malevolent roadblocks to simply getting from one place to another.

Since conflict is at the heart of story, could you add some characters or circumstances that will further delay your hero's progress? A series of complications that aren't traced to the antagonist will provide added surprises for your audience. And, by some clever coincidence, conquering one of these very complications just might provide the exact skill or know-how that comes in handy during the final confrontation.

Chapter 9
ALLIES

"Expansive allies can be drawn into your story to be magnets, drivers, amplifiers capable of broadcasting whatever you decide."
Laurie Perez

A FEW GOOD MENTORS

"When the student is ready the teacher will appear." This is never truer than in fiction, where we've observed countless heroes consulting with that one person who puts them on the path to their ultimate success. This figure may be in the story only briefly, or they may be a trusted companion who gets more than a single scene in which to convey their wisdom to the hero, teach them a new skill, or give them a special item they will use at a critical point in their adventure.

If you mention *Homer's Odyssey* to today's audience, there's a fair chance many of them will think it's an episode of The Simpsons. But it is that Greek classic and its companion work *The Iliad*—written in the 8th century—which introduced the character who would become the namesake for all mentors to come.

In *The Odyssey*, the wise teacher Mentor was inhabited by the goddess Athena. Similarly, in *The Iliad*, her mutually divine brother Apollo serves as a mentor to the upstart Hermes. Following this Grecian formula, mentors throughout the literary ages have often been gifted with supernatural powers.

Wizards in particular tend to populate epics. Merlin, Gandalf and Dumbledore have all been magical advisors to younger wards who have a destiny to fulfill. Meanwhile, their fairer-sex counterparts—fairies—have accommodated the gentler needs of Cinderella, Sleeping Beauty and Pinocchio.

Science fiction mentors frequently possess abilities beyond

those of mere mortals, from *The Matrix's* Morpheus to the little green Jedi master who sounds like Miss Piggy. In such futuristic settings, we readily suspend disbelief and buy their mysterious, godlike qualities.

But because most novels take place in the real world, a typical mentor is a bit more down-to-earth; simply very good at what they do and more experienced than our hero. You gotta love Doc Brown from *Back to the Future*, whose absent-minded professor qualities made him both funny and approachable. And who doesn't get a kick out of *The Karate Kid*'s Mr Miyagi?

Not that all mentors are looking out for our hero's best interests. Melanie Griffith's boss in *Working Girl*, *Wall Street's* Gordon Gekko, and Tom Cruise's bosses in *The Firm* all were out for themselves rather than their younger underlings. But even in these dysfunctional pairings, the hero ends up gaining just as much by learning what *not* to do. Take *Private Benjamin*. Judy's commanding officer was bent on seeing her fail, but as in so many military tales, this only helped Judy find the inner strength to prevail.

For showing us how to help our heroes be heroes, we are thankful for all the fictional mentors who've given ruby slippers to lost little girls, helped jungle boys escape from singing orangutans, and taught home run honeys that there's no crying in baseball.

THAT'S WHAT FRIENDS ARE FOR

Writers have recognized the value of a "second banana" long before vaudeville coined the term (after a skit in which friends share two bananas). Audiences love a good friendship, and writers love it even more because it paves a ready path for:

1) Exposition
2) Plot Progression
3) Conflict
4) Mentoring

RIGHT BRAIN WRITING

In fiction, a writer's best friend can be the friend they give their protagonist. Far from playing second fiddle in the story, a well-crafted companion can open the door for revealing interaction and dialogue. Instead of banging the audience over the head with facts, details conveyed comfortably in a conversation feel perfectly natural, and can even disguise their eventual importance to the story.

In Veronica Roth's blockbuster *Divergent* series, the first friend Tris makes when entering the intimidating new world she has chosen is fellow initiate Christina. Roth cleverly chose to make Christina a "Candor", whose outspoken observations are a steady source of revelation and discovery.

Even Tom Hanks' stranded hero in *Cast Away* is given a volleyball to talk to. His four years on a desert island would have seen him talking to himself without "Wilson" to keep him company. A hero with no one to interact with doesn't reveal much.

In a comedy, it's especially important to have a partner in crime—a foil perhaps—to share the hero's dilemma, or even make it worse. For example, roping a coworker into pretending to be the heroine's fiancé is the sort of ruse from which both companions stand to win or lose, increasing the stakes for all.

Where would Mayberry's Andy have been without Barney? Lucy without Ethel? Those two examples epitomize two very classic chemistries: 1) The sensible protagonist with the wacky friend, and 2) The wacky protagonist with the sensible friend (although Ethel usually could be roped into any hare-brained scheme)

The supporting cast is a rich field for mining useful and very memorable characters. The quirky neighbor is a particularly popular archetype. Sitcoms *Bewitched* and *Three's Company* were enhanced by the nosey neighbor Gladys Kravitz and the befuddled landlord Mr Roper. Viewers of *Newhart* eagerly anticipated the appearance of Larry, Darryl and their other brother Darryl, a trio of country bumpkins in sharp contrast to Bob's button-down personality. Indeed, variety is a major component in the supporting casts of everything from *The Big Bang Theory* to *The Office*.

Looking again at the Mertzes and the Nortons, neighbors have always been a staple of story. In more recent memory, Seinfeld's Kramer opened the door to at least momentary mayhem whenever he came bursting in, just as Lenny and Squiggy did on *Laverne & Shirley*.

Not that all neighbors need to be nutty. Sometimes—as on *Home Improvement*—the guy next door is the voice of reason, even when the fence obscures his informative face.

Whether they are a harbinger of hassles for the hero, or just someone to reveal plot points to, a second banana or a supporting character with pizzazz has the potential to become a breakout personality the audience comes to enjoy on a par with the hero himself.

We put a great deal of thought into our protagonist, making sure they have charisma and wit, and are interesting and worth caring about. Don't they deserve a good friend to hang out with?

OPPOSITES ATTRACT

Conflict makes any story a story, and the most obvious conflict is the one between the protagonist and his obstacle. But an easy and easily overlooked source of conflict is contrast, which can often be found in the hero's own best friend.

If we think of the great duos in the history of entertainment, contrast is easy to spot. Laurel & Hardy, Fred & Barney, Ralph Kramden & Ed Norton feature large heroes who will never be confused with their counterpart. But the contrast doesn't end in the big and tall shop. The hero is often loud and blustering compared to his mild-mannered companion. The mismatch makes for subtle but effective conflict.

A partnership of young and old can provide rich contrast. In the pairing of *Back to the Future*'s Marty McFly and Doc Brown, we get not just an age difference but the collaboration of a high-schooler who needs help and an offbeat professor who knows just enough to get them both in trouble. In the end, the teen's cleverness and the elder's expertise combine to save the day.

You don't have to look far to find conflict in a romance, where the mere pairing of a male and a female creates an underlying battle of the sexes. Has there ever been a romcom where the heroes didn't start off on a bad foot?

Even the music world has discovered that the audience has an ear for contrast. What sick genius came up with the idea of partnering Bing Crosby and David Bowie to record a Christmas single and a holiday TV special? More recently, the pairing of crooner Tony Bennett and the flamboyant Lady Gaga for an album of duets was called "a match made in Heaven" by MTV.

If you're Sherlock Holmes, it's helpful to have a Dr Watson to throw enigmatic observations to. The befuddled companion who comes along for the ride readily allows for exposition that comes naturally as the two discuss evaluations from their own perspectives.

In a nutshell, conflict isn't just found in the great quest or in a lover's spat. A partnership with two unlikely companions offers an undercurrent of contrast that creates friendly tension.

ALL IN THE FAMILY

Author Richard Kelly literally wrote the book on *The Andy Griffith Show*. His highly entertaining and informative volume by that same title is not only a comprehensive episode guide, but a fascinating behind-the-scenes visit with the legendary cast and characters who populated Mayberry from 1960 to 1968.

Some years ago, I had the pleasure of speaking with Richard, and while discussing what made *The Andy Griffith Show* an enduring classic, two things he had to say have always stuck with me, and I've seen their truth time and again:

1. It wasn't about the jokes, but the personalities.
2. The personalities represented the family unit.

To explain:

1. Think of any scene in any episode of *The Andy Griffith Show*. You'll be hard pressed to remember any punchlines. There was plenty of humor, yes, and a spate of catch phrases like "Nip it" or "Gol-ly," but the laughs sprang from the characters and how they dealt with each situation in this situation comedy.

Anticipating how Barney would react to an embarrassing turn of events was often much funnier than any one-liner he might have uttered. We got to know the personalities on the show through their believable, consistent behavior. If it had been a town of stand-up comics, we'd have never bought into it or felt like we knew these people.

That is a failing of many of today's sitcoms, which are a series of setup and punchline, setup and punchline. But back in Mayberry, we cared about Aunt Bee's feelings when the pickles which she thought were prize-winning actually tasted like kerosene.

2. A sense of family invites us in and makes us feel at home. Andy, the patriarch, was complemented by Bee, the mother figure, and of course Opie rounded out the immediate family. We also have characters whose roles approximate the blowhard brother-in-law (Barney), the lovable uncle (Floyd), the busybody aunt (Clara), the unsophisticated cousin (take your pick, Gomer or Goober), and so on. Stereotypes to a large degree, perhaps, but consider other successful sitcoms and you'll see the same formula played out.

A shrewd variation on that theme was *The Mary Tyler Moore Show*. Mary's boss, Lou Grant, was a strong father figure to Mary's career woman of the '70s. (Being the '70s, it was cool not to have kids, but if there was a child on the show, wide-eyed Georgette might fill the bill.) Ted Baxter was your blustering brother-in-law, and Murray was the uncle you could go to for a different view on things.

Again, most of the characters on this show had personalities we got to know, to the point where humor could come from merely expecting how they would react to situations.

A good one-liner is fine for a quick laugh. But for humor that reaches the heart and stays with us, a situation we can identify with and a personality we care about is the magic formula. Andy had that magic, which is why there will always be a fondness for Mayberry.

HOW MANY CHARACTERS DOES IT TAKE?

We've all heard the old joke, "How many (fill-in-the-blank) does it take to change a lightbulb?" There are countless permutations, but one of my favorites is:

"How many mystery writers does it take to change a light bulb?"

"Two. One to screw it almost all the way in and the other to give it a twist at the end."

The question we will ponder as we get into casting our story is another one to do with quantity: *How many characters does my story need?*

Perhaps fewer than you think. A play I once attended was performed by a single solitary actress. Something about a trip to Europe, as I recall. What I remember most is that, as part of the story, she actually fried up real bacon and eggs on stage, to enticingly aromatic effect. (I was glad I had eaten beforehand or it might have turned into a two-person play.)

Similarly, Hal Halbrook entertained audiences for six decades with his one-man show *Mark Twain Tonight*. From these examples, it might seem as though a single character can be sufficient for a full-length story, which is indeed sometimes the case. More often than not, however, their narratives include numerous anecdotes that do involve other people.

A sprawling Dickens novel, on the other hand, weaves in a

generous cast of characters. *David Copperfield* and *Oliver Twist*, for example, include roles for ten major players each, with some of these sub-characters becoming more famous than the protagonist himself. Only Ebeneezer Scrooge seems to have surpassed his cast.

There are over fifty characters in the *Lord of the Rings* saga. Thank goodness we don't have to keep track of every one of them. Maintaining a working knowledge of the comings and goings of the ten-plus main characters while traversing the 455,125 words in this trilogy takes some doing as it is.

That said, from classic dramas like *Twelve Angry Men* and *The Dirty Dozen* to campy comedies like *It's a Mad, Mad, Mad, Mad World* (which crammed in as many celebrities of the day as the budget allowed), audiences have proven that they can handle a handful. The more recent *The Hateful Eight* and the fact that the latest *Ocean's 11* film has been scaled down to *Ocean's 8* does seem to suggest a trend toward slightly smaller ensembles, but who's counting.

Ideally, we don't want to have so many characters that the reader gets confused. At the same time, a well-rounded ensemble full of distinctive personalities offers variety and keeps the hero from having to do all the heavy lifting.

By its nature, a love story is going to need a minimum of two characters. A mystery novel, on the other hand, benefits from a large enough cast to provide sufficient suspects. In general, there's no need to include "utility" characters in your head count (such as a store clerk or a flight attendant) unless they have a significant or recurring role.

A logical answer to our original question could well depend on how complex the story is, how long it may be, and whether the length provides for some resolution for each of the major players. A short story only allows for one or two problems to solve, which can be accomplished with a minimal cast. If there are a dozen heroes, companions, and enemies to address, more pages will be necessary to sort it all out and provide closure for each of the primary characters. (Secondary and incidental characters can likely slide.)

Every character has their own story to tell, and each one you add becomes one more in the bigger picture. So, as you may have already concluded, the simple answer to the question of how many characters you need is: Exactly as many it takes to tell your story.

THE NAME GAME

Regardless of the population in your plot, care should be taken to choose names that are distinct. A story that includes both a Carol and a Carolyn is begging to confuse the reader. It's amazing how often this simple rule is overlooked.

An author friend and I once got on the subject of interesting names, including those of real people. Among the monikers that came up in our conversation were Piers Tilbury and Thurl Ravenscroft. In case you don't recognize those names, I'll tell you who they are momentarily.

But first, don't you get an immediate, unique feeling from each of these names? Doesn't Piers Tilbury convey a certain regality? Doesn't Thurl Ravenscroft sound intimidating, like someone straight out of Hogwarts?

I won't keep you in suspense. Piers Tilbury is a talented artist in the UK who specializes in fiction book covers. And Thurl Ravenscroft—whose voice was as formidable as his name—did many deep-throated vocal characterizations for Disney, sang the Christmas classic "You're a Mean One, Mr Grinch", and for over fifty years hawked Frosted Flakes as the voice of Tony the Tiger.

Think about it. Boris Karloff is a name that overflows with menace, even if you've never seen *Frankenstein* or his other creepy roles. (His real name, by the way, was William Pratt.) Likewise, cowboy actor Marion Morrison knew his name wouldn't hold up in a saloon showdown, and promptly changed it to John Wayne. What a simple, All-American frontier sort of name.

As we brainstorm names for the characters in our stories, it does help readers remember them by making them a good fit; perhaps even one that reinforces the role of the character.

Going back to Hogwarts for a moment, doesn't Harry Potter's Professor Severus Snape sound every bit as imposing as the Dark Arts master it belongs to? And doesn't Holly Golightly from *Breakfast at Tiffany's* suggest a free spirit who doesn't take life very seriously?

Which is not to say that a less assuming name doesn't have merit. Sometimes it may even be preferable, to make a certain character as forgettable as possible. In some whodunnits, this has been used effectively to avert the reader from the ultimate culprit.

Ian Fleming turned a forgettable name into a phenomenon. He explained, "One of the bibles of my youth was 'Birds of the West Indies' by James Bond, a well-known ornithologist, and when I was casting about for a name for my protagonist I thought, 'My God, that's the dullest name I've ever heard.' So I appropriated it. Now the dullest name in the world has become an exciting one." Indeed, if 007 had been given a name like Ace McPistol, it would be much harder for him to work undercover.

Just like you give your characters interesting backstories, give them a name that goes well with their personality. No one will fault you for using normal, everyday names like Bob Smith or Jane Jones, but something in between plain vanilla and Black Forest Pistachio Chip Ripple might give your story some extra flavors.

NAMES IN THE MAGIC MIRROR

When *Romper Room* (1953-1994) was on the air, many regions had their own version of this kiddie show using a local TV host. Mine had "Miss Jean".

I remember little about the show itself beyond its signature segment, in which the host held up a "magic mirror" and recited these words:

RIGHT BRAIN WRITING

Romper, Bomper, Stomper, Boo
Tell me, tell me, tell me, do
Magic Mirror, tell me today
Have all my friends had fun at play?

After this incantation, each regional host would look at the camera and recite the first names of a handful of children in her viewing audience ("I see Jimmy, and I see Cindy..."). Presumably these were the kids whose parents had written in on their behalf. Maybe she supplemented with random names for good measure. Even at my young age I considered that possibility, though it was still a mild thrill if she happened to speak my name, and those moments did feel a bit magical.

Spreading similar joy to the other end of the age spectrum, weatherman Willard Scott took it a step further on *The Today Show* when he would congratulate someone on their 90th or 100th birthday and show their photo (brought to you by Smucker's). It's a fair guess that these nonagenarians and centenarians got the same thrill as *Romper Room's* preschoolers did at the mention of their name, age and city.

Those simple factoids to identify strangers are often our own starting point when we're creating characters for our story. We usually begin with basic details like their name. We have a general sense of their age, and we envision them in a particular setting. But, like Miss Jean or Mr Scott, we don't know much about them until we fill in some essential details.

For this reason, writers often work up a fact sheet, chronicling such details as the characters' physical features like their hair color, eye color, height, weight, race, education, place of birth, etc. Some authors go so far as to include mannerisms, pet phrases, quirks, whether the character has an accent, and so on. This tactic is helpful and comes in especially handy if there are multiple characters to keep track of.

That said, a fact sheet provides little more than a sketch of the character. That's when many authors dig deeper to flesh out their character by exploring his/her motivations, belief system, hopes, and fears. What childhood incident left an emotional scar? What achievements give them strength? What have been the turning points in their life? Answering questions like these brings our stick figure character to life by giving him a soul.

You'll want to include irony and conflict in your character's psyche; that is, who they want to be versus what is inside holding them back. Often they are their own biggest hurdle. As author/philosopher Albert Camus said, "Man is the only creature who refuses to be what he is."

A writer who has clearly tuned into their protagonist rarely regrets having invested the time to do so. The result is an authentic and well-defined character qualified to mirror the magic of your story.

GOOD GOSSIP

Oscar Wilde once said, "If there is anything more annoying in the world than having people talk about you, it is certainly having no one talk about you."

I suppose that depends on what they're saying, of course.

But nowhere does gossip serve a more helpful purpose than in fiction. If our heroes are lucky, there are plenty of other characters talking about them behind their backs.

In fiction, there is much to gain from hearsay, and I'm here to say it. Among the benefits:

Backstory

Right along with Ebenezer Scrooge, we learn the reasons why he grew up to be a lonely old miser via ghosts who show him pivotal moments from his life. During those scenes, characters reveal their opinions of him to one another. This is much more dramatic than if the ghosts had simply told Scrooge why no one likes him.

When we first saw Forrest Gump, we wondered what his deal was. It was enlightening to hear conversations about his medical history like those between his mother and his doctor.

Exposition

At the beginning of a story, we are just getting to know the main character. But his/her companions and associates have known them for a long time and have a strong sense of who they are. We are brought up to speed in short order by parents who worry about their son's choice of friends or teachers complaining about the new principal's track record.

Glimpses of trouble ahead are well served by coworkers spreading rumors, or when the evil adversary spells out to accomplices how the hero's vulnerabilities will be exploited.

Reaction

When a bride-to-be tells a friend of her engagement, she may receive an enthusiastic congratulations, and we assume everyone's happy. But we become privy to the spinster friend's real reaction when she spews a jealous diatribe to a mutual acquaintance.

Or perhaps the groom-to-be didn't propose at all, and a misunderstanding grew too big to get out of. The behind-the-scenes conversations between him and his best man tell the real story of what he's going through. The truth comes out, and it can provide an interesting turn of events when it does.

In *The Invention of Lying*, we saw how brutal honesty can hurt when it's told face to face. In a perfect world, apparently, a little subterfuge can actually be a good thing.

In the all-knowing, all-seeing eyes of fiction, there are no secrets. Enjoy exposing your characters' underlying mysteries and exploiting the salacious scuttlebutt.

But you didn't hear it from me.

A DAZZLING CHARACTER DEVELOPMENT TRICK

"Little kids just don't get magic."

That's been said by many a birthday party magician, and it's easy to understand why. At a young age, children have yet to differentiate the natural world from the supernatural world. Taking things at face value, the incongruity of a rabbit suddenly appearing from a hat is beyond their scope. They're more interested in the rabbit itself.

I got a first-hand taste of this years ago doing the one magic trick I know. Actually, it's not even magic, and it's barely a trick. Using the most elementary of skills, I can make it look like I've removed my thumb from one hand while it wiggles in the other. I haven't fooled any adults with it, and older kids groan at its lameness. But I will never forget the reaction of a kindergartener who ran off in terror, horrified that I took off a finger. Thank goodness I didn't saw someone in half.

As we know, children have a simpler view of the world than adults. So we wouldn't write a scene with a couple of seven-year-olds discussing quantum physics or amortization schedules. But we may be less aware of the characteristic degrees of development our adult characters can also express.

At each stage in life, people's wants and needs change. Behaviorists have given us some insights we can take advantage of if we really want to get into the heads of our characters.

One useful resource is Richard Barrett's *"The Stages of Psychological Development"*. Barrett provides us with an explanation of each stage of our age at www.barrettacademy.com/stages-of-psychological-development.

It's rather heady stuff, but quite eye-opening and worth a look. For our purposes, here is an oversimplification:

BIRTH TO TWO YEARS
Surviving, having needs met

TWO TO EIGHT YEARS
Conforming, seeking love and acceptance

EIGHT TO 24 YEARS
Respect and recognition, displaying looks or talent to become part of a group

25 TO 39 YEARS
Individuating, becoming oneself through expressing values and autonomy

40 TO 49 YEARS
Self-actualizing, becoming oneself through expressing gifts and talents

50 TO 59 YEARS
Integrating, collaborating with others and making a difference

60+ YEARS
Selfless serving, social justice, leaving a legacy

These won't apply to everyone—nor every character—but could any of these underlying needs add an extra dimension to your protagonists and those they encounter? Perhaps your 55-year-old shop owner who does sleuthing on the side is also the president of a civics organization…an ideal way to introduce an entire cast of red herrings.

Knowing each character's stage of development is handy for giving them individuality. Researching their motivations in depth can also help you rely less on clichés and find layers to their personality that might surprise even you.

WRITING YOUR CHARACTERS' TRUE FEELINGS

A favorite couple of mine has a youngster who loves to role-play, so whenever I visit we play this little game.

"Make an angry face," I say. He frowns.

"Make a surprised face." His eyes and mouth open wide.

"Make a scary face." He narrows his eyes and shows his teeth.

We keep this going either until I run out of emotions or *Spongebob Squarepants* comes on, but I always try to end the game with a happy face.

Even when it isn't part of a game, it's easy to read what kind of mood a preschooler is in. It's once we grow up that we are prone to conceal our feelings and make them less visible to others. When dealing with adults, what you see isn't always what you get.

Writing a character's emotions via obvious physical cues alone rarely hits the mark, especially if they are clichés. A character whose "heart leaps" at the sight of her beloved or who has "tear-stained cheeks" implodes with unoriginality. Something as rich and personal as *feelings* deserves better.

Crocodile Tears

We've all gotten them, thanks to a well-meaning relative or a friend who doesn't know us very well: a forwarded email sharing a supposedly touching story that you absolutely must read.

Never mind that it usually ends with, "If you have a heart, you'll send this to twelve people you love." Or that in most cases, a quick check on Snopes.com will verify that this "true" story—like too many forwards—is completely bogus.

Even more offensive is the uncredited writer's weak attempt at conjuring emotion out of us merely by stating that one of the characters *cried*. How many times have we read lines like these toward the climax of one of these tepid tales:

"With tear-stained cheeks, she thanked the kind stranger."

"With a tear in his eye, the panhandler accepted the old woman's last quarter."

"Choking back the tears, he..." Oh, knock it off already.

These stories are so artificially heartwarming, they're almost flammable. Whoever originates these anonymous forwards has an uncanny knack for overestimating their ability to create emotion through story, to the point where they must wave a flag and show that this moment is supposed to be touching.

So how do we create emotion in a story so that the reader feels it, instead of just our overemotional characters?

It's what's inside that counts

Focus not on what's visible through outside appearance, but rather by revealing what's going on *inside*. What is our character really thinking? What is their behavior that makes them unique?

For example, it's obvious that someone will worry if they think they may have left the stove on after leaving the house. But going deeper, every individual has a thought process all their own. One person may head back home in a panic, another may blame their spouse and start an argument, while another may eventually write it off and let fate decide.

What your character thinks and what they do in response to a situation reveals much more than a tear-stained cheek will. Instead of focusing on the obvious, use the moment to dramatic advantage. Eliminate extraneous words in phrases like "tears in her eyes" or "furrowed eyebrows". (Where else would we have tears, and where else would we have furrows?)

Writers also create moods with setting; perhaps the most blatant and overused—but still effective—being rain when the hero's future is suddenly gloomy. Empty or broken objects in the scene are oft-used reflections of the hero's potentially lost cause. There is much that can parallel the circumstance and suggest "this is sad" besides tears.

Not that our characters can't cry, of course. Giving them true-to-life personalities demands that they are capable of waterworks. We simply should save it for moments of genuine anguish. If our heroine becomes inconsolable because she lost her wedding ring, how will we top that emotion later when her mother dies? Save that beat for when you really need it.

A savvy reader will pick up on inappropriate and overblown character reactions. Sometimes it's best to let the scene speak for itself and let the reader decide how sad they think things are.

In the words of Lemony Snicket:

"When someone is crying, of course, the noble thing to do is to comfort them. But if someone is trying to hide their tears, it may also be noble to pretend you do not notice them."

Regardless of whether a smile, frown or other physical display accompanies them, feelings are a very *internal* thing. When writing emotions, seek out the more secretive elements of that very human experience. Coming up with a scene that touches the heart authentically will circumvent fake fiction and elicit a more genuine reaction from your reader.

WHAT DO YOUR CHARACTERS WANT?

Whether Mick Jagger knew it or not, he immortalized one of the great rules of fiction writing when he came up with "You can't always get what you want." If our characters don't have difficulty getting what they deeply desire, there isn't much to write about.

Oliver Twist and Little Orphan Annie wanted a family. The Little Mermaid wanted to discover the world beyond her sea. The bedridden writer in Stephen King's *Misery* wanted to escape the crazy lady with the sledgehammer.

Conflict being at the heart of good storytelling, the bigger the hero's dream, the bigger the obstacle should be. If we can put enough impediments in their way that it seems impossible to reach the goal, the reader will have no choice but to stick around to find out how this miracle will take place.

Occasionally we have a hero with no immediate needs, for whom everything is smooth sailing. In those cases, it's time to rock the boat by throwing them a curveball. We give them a problem that forces them to want to fix things.

To up the stakes, we include an antagonist whose wants are in direct opposition to the hero's goals. Sometimes they are adversaries from the beginning; other times they don't even know each other or the fact that they're competing until well into the story. In both cases, we often keep them separated physically for as long as possible, building up to a climactic final confrontation.

While it's tempting to focus on the two characters involved in the main conflict, we open up additional levels of interest if we remember that everybody wants something, including all of the minor characters. In the minds of every one of them, *they* are the protagonist of your story.

Even those who appear for only one scene have motivations of their own. The receptionist who is inconvenienced by the hero's pursuit of her boss, the night watchman who wants to know why the hero is loitering after hours, and the TV reporter who spins a report to suit their agenda are all opportunities to move the story along with microconflicts.

While keeping the complications coming, a good rhythm of ebb and flow teases the audience with one step forward, two steps back, and creates an atmosphere of "Will they make it or not?"

As in real life, the hero's main goal is merely one of countless other objectives happening simultaneously. *The Hunger Games'* Katniss Everdeen doesn't just want to survive, she wants to protect her family, be with her true love, punish the oppressor, achieve world peace, etc. Multilayered motivation makes for a well-rounded, more believable character, and compounding the obstacles they face heightens the drama.

We all want a happy ending. But in fiction, the real joy is in the journey and the conflicts along the way.

HOW TO GET INSIDE YOUR CHARACTER'S HEAD

"If you could read my mind," Gordon Lightfoot once sang, "what a tale my thoughts could tell." We may approach a story that we write as one single story, but it has more layers for readers to enjoy when we take advantage of the fact that each of our characters has his or her own hidden history.

As kids, playing make believe was fun and effortless, and psychologists confirm that it's good for us. At Halloween, some contend that the choice of costume is an extension of one's inner self. Others observe that costumes frequently suggest the opposite personality of the wearer. Either way, it's a chance to step outside of ourselves for a little while.

As grownups, role playing doesn't come as naturally, but the business world has made it more acceptable. Using it for training purposes, employees are given the opportunity to make mistakes without suffering real world consequences. The roles they play may even find them acting as someone they don't want to be, like an irate customer, to better understand another person's point of view.

Which is why writers especially can benefit from pretending to be someone we're not. Every character we create becomes three-dimensional if we get inside their heads. While it's tempting to grab a stereotype and run with something we know to be safe and proven, the most memorable characters of literature have been anything but cardboard cutouts.

So how do we unlock those secrets deep inside our fictional friends? Here are five easy pathways to perception.

Feel the Fear

Knowing your character's primary goal for the story (finding the right mate, conquering an enemy, winning a case), imagine the worst that can happen to them. What will be the consequences if they fail? What obstacles can you put in place to make it all but impossible to succeed?

Not feeling their pain yet? Up the stakes by giving them an internal struggle in direct conflict with their goal. Claustrophobia could be a roadblock for a race car driver. A med student with a queasy stomach also has demons to contend with. Remember, there is wonderful irony afoot when someone is their own biggest obstacle.

Grill Them

One by one, sit your heroes, villains, and other significant characters across from you in a virtual chair and play doctor. Dr

Sigmund Freud, that is. Or Dr Joyce Brothers. Or Dr Ruth, if you dare. Ask your character probing questions about their life, their background, their goals, etc. But don't stop there. Get really personal with them and ask *why* they became a brain surgeon, *why* they want to be a rock star, *why* they promised themselves to see the world before they're 30.

But don't stop there either. Keep digging deeper until you uncover the real reason why it's a matter of life and death to them that they succeed in their goals. Persist, because they'll be as evasive about revealing their true selves as you are. Be Barbara Walters and make them cry if you have to. Don't worry, they'll forgive you.

Consult an Expert

Your circle of friends and acquaintances is an extravaganza of information and personal experience to help with your character development. Is your hero a policeman? A mailman? A dental hygienist? Someone you know or someone they know would be glad to help you connect with the inner workings of your character.

In the name of full disclosure, you may want to tell them ahead of time that it's for literary accuracy. They'll be more open and inclined to tell all. I once pummeled a nurse friend with an inquisition about hospital procedure until she accused, "You're doing research for a book, aren't you?"

Immerse Yourself

Walk a mile in your character's shoes. If he or she has a penchant for gambling, spend a day at a casino. If they have a green thumb, get your fingers dirty in the garden or hang out at a nursery. If they are a beach bum, I can think of worse things than sipping piña coladas in a hammock for the sake of research.

Listen Through Their Ears

Just like you, your character has very individual taste in

music. Would he/she listen to pop tunes, oldies, heavy metal, country, soul, hip-hop, classical? Who are his or her favorite artists? While you're pondering your character's modus operandi, tune into their type of station or call up the genre on a free service like AccuRadio.com. Filmmaker Quentin Tarantino says he'll go so far as to make a mix tape to the tune of his characters.

Or maybe your story takes place in a different time period. Someone in the 1940s was hearing big band music. Two decades earlier, ragtime was the bee's knees. If your story takes place in a foreign setting, music from that region makes an ideal soundtrack for your writing.

Any of these activities can help a writer hone in on the protagonist, antagonist, and anyone else in the cast. Of course, being the brilliant and imaginative wordsmiths we are, we can simply create our characters to be whomever we want them to be. But how much more fun is it when they instead reveal themselves to us?

Section IV

KEEPING IT REAL

Chapter 10
DIALOGUE

"Writing dialogue is the only respectable way of contradicting yourself. I put a position, rebut it, refute the rebuttal, and rebut the refutation."

Tom Stoppard

ALL TALK AND NO ACTION

Word guy that I am, I like to turn on the subtitles when I'm watching TV. Number one, there are too many celebrities who mumble. Number two, I find it interesting to see how the words on the screen are interpreted by the actors. And three, it can be funny when a news channel with auto-translation thinks "senior advisor" is "seen your abs eyesore."

There are other times when I will close my eyes and just listen. Lacking visual cues, I assess how effectively the dialogue alone carries the story. I am frequently surprised by the lengthy breaks of no dialogue at all, when wordless action takes over, especially during movies.

These scenarios illustrate how dialogue and action depend on each other. In a book, long pauses like the one above will be covered by narrative, explaining the silent activity taking place or providing exposition. A novel with an abundance of dialogue benefits from reprieves from incessant conversation. Even though the reader is still consuming a litany of words, they do not register in the same audible way.

By the same token, too much narrative without quality exchanges of dialogue gets wearisome. We like to see dialogue coming because we think communicatively, whether it's conversation with friends or our own endless inner monologue (we see something out of the ordinary and literally think to ourselves, "What's that?").

Deciding what to say via dialogue and what to say via narration becomes easier by remembering this classic saying:

"If you can't say something right, don't say it at all."

Okay, I changed that a bit. But in writing dialogue, it's more important to say something *right* than to say something nice.

Dialogue is "wrong" when it's unrealistic and doesn't ring true.

In normal conversation, people don't talk in long, uninterrupted diatribes. Jack Nicholson's famous "You can't handle the truth" monologue works because the setting is a courtroom interrogation and he happens to be on the stand. Plus, he's Jack Nicholson. Most of all, the entire preceding story is structured to lead up to his climactic soliloquy.

Dialogue feels especially unnatural when characters give awkward exposition:

"Hi, dear brother! I haven't seen you since Aunt Grace's funeral in Minneapolis two years ago this August."

or:

"Did Leonard's family get here yet?"

"Yes, around 3:00," she answered, "with an entourage that included his wife, two noisy, badly-behaved children and several suitcases big enough to tote tubas in."

Instead, let the narration do the heavy lifting:

"Yes, around 3," she answered, "with a couple of spoiled brats." She recalled the oversized suitcases they had brought in and imagined stuffing the children in them.

Don't load too much exposition on your character's back. Simply put, if a real person wouldn't say it, neither should your character.

That said, dialogue is "wrong" if it's *too* realistic.

Between typical people, conversation includes a lot of stuff that would run a reader off:

"Did you take out the trash?"
"Yeah."
"Did you remember to take out the recycles?"
"Yeah."
"Even the stuff I had by the door?"
"Yeah."
"Okay."

or:

"I'll see you tomorrow."
"Okay, what time?"
"I dunno, how about 2:00?"
"Can we make it 2:30?"
"Sure."
"Great. Thanks."
"No problem. See you tomorrow."

Minutia like this is the stuff of life, but not the stuff of story. Any dialogue that doesn't further the plot doesn't belong. Readers conditioned to a snappy pace don't think twice when a character says something dramatic and simply leaves. But they do take note if dialogue lapses into banality.

Dialogue becomes a thing of beauty when it delivers the unexpected. Instead of:

"I saw Grace at the supermarket today."
"Yeah? How is she?"

How about:

"I saw Grace at the supermarket today."
"Grace is in Italy."

Dialogue done right can be just as intriguing as your action scenes. Put some well-crafted dialogue in the mouths of your characters, and you'll give your readers something to talk about.

NEVER CAN SAY GOODBYE

On a related note, it's especially amusing that characters in movies and on TV don't end their phone calls with any sort of "goodbye". They invariably say the last thing they have to say and then just hang up.

In real life, hanging up the phone without a farewell would literally leave your other party hanging. They'd think they got cut off, or spend the rest of the day wondering whether they'd said something wrong.

In fiction, however, audiences have no qualms with it. The real-world courtesy of a farewell only serves to bog down the dramatic works. Consider the difference between these two phone conversations:

"How many bodies are there?"
"Three."
It took Spangler a moment to collect the right words.
"Is one of them a redhead?"
"Yes."
"I was afraid of that."
Spangler closed his phone and reached for his coat.

Versus:

"How many bodies are there?"
"Three."
It took Spangler a moment to collect the right words.
"Is one of them a redhead?"
"Yes."
"I was afraid of that. Okay, I'm on my way."
"Okay, bye."
"Bye."
Spangler closed his phone and reached for his coat.

The triviality of the closing exchange is almost comical in comparison, since there are much more important things going on for anyone to engage in niceties. Of course, if the scene is about two lovers having late-night pillow talk via phone, a dreamy "Goodnight" is more than appropriate and reinforces the mood. Hopefully there are no bodies involved.

Hanging up the phone with words unspoken isn't the only device writers use to end a conversation on the strongest note. Scenes or chapters often end on a pivotal piece of dialogue, never miring in anticlimactic follow-up verbiage.

Next time you see a character answer the phone, I think you'll be amused at how unrealistically he or she ends the call. But in drama it's the way things are done, and it works. We take it at face value because the characters do too.

GET OUT OF MY HEAD

You've probably heard the saying that "relationships are mirrors," which is a fascinating notion. There's something reassuring in the concept that the people around us are put there to teach us things about ourselves.

When we're with people we admire or enjoy, we recognize the positive traits we want to cultivate within ourselves. Perhaps we gain even more by taking note of things we don't appreciate in other people, making a conscious effort not to "be like that."

In some respects, we are human sponges. When we spend a

lot of time in the company of an acquaintance, it's not uncommon to catch ourselves echoing some of their characteristics. We pick up on their traits, sharing inside jokes and repeating some of their pet expressions. In life, that has a certain charm to it, being a bonding experience between two people.

But in writing dialogue, pet phrases are something to be careful with. The audience expects characters to have well-defined, separate personalities, and failing to monitor that is a writing mistake too easily and too often made. To explain:

In a scene from a recent hit movie, one of the characters made the sarcastic comment, "I can't wait." A few scenes later, an unrelated character, in totally different circumstances, made the sarcastic comment, "I can't wait." The second time around was a little distracting. (Not that two people can't say the same thing on the same day, but it did seem a tad coincidental. For now, we'll give them the benefit of the doubt.)

Then, this past week on a popular TV comedy, a main character made reference to an object as having a "vibe" to it. Not ten seconds later in the next scene, an unaffiliated character said dialogue that included the expression "vibe". That seemed a little too coincidental, and the impression one gets is that someone wasn't paying a lot of attention to making these characters distinct from one another. You're suddenly brought back to reality (and out of the story) by the realization that a writer wrote these words and they must have been fond of a particular phrase that day.

While it's within the realm of backstory possibility that these characters "knew" each other and therefore could have absorbed each other's vibe (sorry), it's highly unlikely that the writer had that in mind, and we sure didn't.

Despite the fact that he was best friends with Fred Flintstone, you'd never hear Barney Rubble exclaim "Yabba-Dabba-Doo". Therefore, the "sponge" factor has no place in fiction, and we must take care to expunge the sponge from our own writing.

At the same time, *intentional* mirroring of phrases can be a powerful tool. Anyone who's seen *The Princess Bride* will recall the brilliant, touching use of "As you wish."

Imitation may be the sincerest form of flattery, but characters saying the same things is sincerely confusing. Let each line of dialogue speak for itself and you can spare your characters some unnecessary identity crises.

RIGHT BRAIN WRITING

Chapter 11
DESCRIPTION

"Fiction is the lie through which we tell the truth."
Albert Camus

SEVEN WAYS TO AVOID AWKWARD EXPOSITION

We've talked about heavy-handed dialogue, the kind that attempts to convey meaningful insight but instead winds up as clumsy elaboration. Well-intended though it may be, painfully purposeful prose will jar an audience out of your fictional magnificence and snap them back to reality.

So how are we supposed to get essential details across without banging readers over the head with blatancy? Here are several ways those who've gone before us have done it:

1. Through the voice of an expert

A detective investigating a crime, a professor teaching a class, or two colleagues having a work discussion all have valid reason to go into details that might not appear in normal conversation. Even then, it's inadvisable to spill everything at once. We've all seen confessions on television shows that were too easily evoked and earnestly explained.

2. As a sidenote

At a wedding in *The Godfather*, Michael Corleone's girlfriend wants to know how it came to be that a famous singer is attending. The resulting story reveals essential workings of the "family business" as well as the power of Michael's don dad. It comes across as a natural extension of the conversation.

3. In the midst of a bigger distraction

In *Jaws*, when shark hunter Quint describes his horrifying

experiences with maneaters to Chief Brody and oceanographer Hooper, it's nighttime in a boat and we're already anticipating toothy Bruce any minute now. We're grateful for not only the opportunity to delay the terror, but also for the informative details that tell us what we're up against.

4. In a hurry

"I only have a minute to tell you this," is a good excuse to unload a lot of info in a short amount of time. In *Back to the Future*, Marty learns about time machines, flux capacitors and plutonium in the time it takes for Libyan terrorists to traverse the mall parking lot.

5. That old favorite, Show Don't Tell

We could either devote unnecessary pages of dialogue to having a wallflower bemoan to her friends that she doesn't hit it off with guys and has a crummy car, or we can write a dramatic scene showing her striking out at a party and getting in a car that won't start.

In an adventure tale involving a superhero or a secret agent, we would rather see their futuristic gadgetry in action than hear about it. If we already knew the Batmobile could turn into a boat, we wouldn't think "how cool is that" when it surprises us.

6. An eye for detail

The scenery itself has its own backstory to tell. A reception area with perfect furniture and fresh flowers says success. A city in ruins spells war. A desk littered with books, papers and cookies means you've seen my office. Don't judge me.

7. Do It Like Disney

Disney wastes no time revealing what the heroine wants. We hear it all in their opening number. While our novel's protagonist may not be able to burst into song, we can give a glimpse into the longings of his or her heart through the actions they take. Checking the want ads, joining a gym, or working on a lab experiment after coworkers all go home give some indication of motivation.

First impressions are among the strongest, which makes the beginning of the story the ideal time to establish traits that can be subtly built upon over the course of the story.

The devil, as they say, may be in the details, but we can ease their arrival by creating non-forced moments in which to position our exposition.

GIVING TOO MUCH AWAY

"Too much information" is known as such for good reason. There is a point at which communicating the facts jumps the fence beyond relevance and becomes overwhelming. TMI can kill conversation, topple empires, and ruin an otherwise good story. Knowing where to draw the line is one of the marks of a savvy storyteller.

Ideally, the reader should never realize they're getting backstory. Here are five proven ways to deliver details with finesse.

1. Be patient

You know everything your reader needs to know and are probably eager to get it out into the open, but the first chapter may not be the place to share the hero's life story. Getting accustomed to the characters, the setting, the mood, and a hint at what the story's about is a lot to take in, so give the audience time to assimilate it. More importantly, give them enough time to *care* about any of it. Once they've become invested in what's going on, they will appreciate learning the finer points.

2. Know when to hold 'em

Kenny Rogers had the right idea in "The Gambler" when he sang of life as a poker game. A well-told story exhibits the same principles of timing and restraint. If there's a lot of backstory, don't spill everything at once. Play your hand strategically and keep the ace up your sleeve for the right moment, when the audience will be most surprised by the revelation.

3. Pick a fight

There's no better way to hide exposition than to distract with drama. Conflict is always interesting, and if the audience is tuned into trouble, they will scarcely notice that they are also learning backstory. An argument at a family reunion can reveal someone's drinking problem or the origins of a grievance between siblings. Compare the heightened energy of such a scene to a placid conversation that covers the same information.

4. Fun with flashbacks

This is an especially popular device used for villains and victims. The killer spots a stranger scolding a child, which triggers the memory of his own father beating him. The girl visits a beach and has visions of herself and her now-deceased boyfriend frolicking in the sand.

5. Get the picture

Gotta pull out the old "show and tell" again here. A picture is worth more than a thousand words if the audience can see for themselves that the heroine is a shoplifter or the attorney is slipped a bribe from the opposing side. Letting the audience figure out some things on their own encourages them to be a participant in the story.

Remember, a discerning reader readily picks up on bungled backstory, so the fewer words it takes to give a history lesson, the better. When it comes to exposition, there's a lot to be said for not saying a lot.

THAT'S NOT WHAT I ASKED

There is a fine line between necessary details and too much

information. Consider how often an exchange like this happens:

Person 1: When are you taking your vacation?
Person 2: Well, we were planning on going in May, but our youngest has soccer tryouts and we need to be here for that. Then my nephew and his wife are coming for a visit to show us the new baby, and . . .

By the time Person 2 gets around to "What was the question again?" Person 1 is sorry they asked.

We all know folks who use the greeting "How are you?" as an invitation to go down the laundry list of ailments and symptoms they've been experiencing. Granted, there are times when we genuinely seek a detailed answer when asking, "How are you?", like when Person 2 is coming out of a coma.

Watching entertainment awards, one can't help but notice the tendency of some winners to give more information than is appropriate. "And the Oscar goes to..." is not asking the question, "What are your thoughts on politics?"

Those on the receiving end of extraneous dissertations are not getting what they asked for, but rather an exercise in patience. In fact, when anything we've anticipated takes a turn out of sync with our expectations, the result is typically disappointment and sometimes resentment. As avid consumers, we are prone to expect a product to be that product with no undue surprises. Which includes books.

A frequent complaint of those who read a lot is their annoyance with novels that go into unneeded backstory or detail about the industry, profession, or region where the story takes place. When it gets to the point where they're skipping pages at a time, they already know they're not going to read that author again.

Bestselling authors reveal that although they may do voluminous research, they make it a point not to put it all in their story. When it's in their head, the essential information will filter onto the page organically, without force-feeding it to the reader.

Giving the audience exactly what they're asking for (a well-worded story that doesn't waste their time) will generate the preferred response when you ask, "What did you think of my book?" That's an answer you'll actually want to hear.

DIDN'T SEE IT COMING

People love surprises when it's something good like an unexpected gift or bumping into an old friend at the grocery store. Other surprises, say an eviction notice or a fender bender, not so much. But one thing readers always enjoy is the element of surprise in a story.

It's no surprise that mystery readers analyze every clue they can find in an attempt to figure out whodunit, and indeed the whole point is to earn the right to say, "I knew it all along." But it's an added bonus if something that didn't even seem like a clue turns out to be a missing link.

However, red herrings needn't be limited to mysteries. Don't you love it when someone who works for the bad guy ends up becoming an ally of the good guy? Turning the tables in a twist that compliments the plot or complicates things for the hero makes a story come alive.

Many a tale has benefited from an important person or prop initially dismissed as inconsequential. A man we thought was a blind beggar warns a young guy about an angry girlfriend he saw enter the apartment building. A birthday bouquet we assumed was sent to a nursing home invalid by her daughter was actually arranged for by a fellow patient.

Another popular technique is to surprise not the reader, but rather the main character. Let the audience know the hero is about to inherit a circus. Reveal that the in-laws are arriving for Thanksgiving a day early in hopes of pleasing the newlyweds. Being in on an upcoming surprise gives the reader omnipotence, and the anticipation of what will happen when the protagonist finds out allows them to be a virtual participant in the story.

Perhaps the most powerful surprise of all is when the ending turns everything upside down and makes you rethink the meaning of the entire story. *The Sixth Sense* and *Planet of the Apes* did that, and I can't help thinking of *Psycho* whenever I think of rethinking.

Predictability has a certain comfort factor to it, but it's the element of surprise that enthralls and keeps readers coming back for more. If you find your story is lacking momentum, inject the unexpected. You may be pleasantly surprised.

THREE'S COMPANY

Everyone knows that if you had a genie in a lamp, he would grant you three wishes. A fair question would be, Why is it always three wishes? The correct answer is: Because the number three is *magic*.

We all grew up on fairy tales and fables that reinforced the number three repeatedly: Goldilocks encountered three bowls of porridge, three chairs, three beds, and, ultimately, three bears. Jack climbed the beanstalk and collected three golden objects. Cinderella had a fairy godmother who evidently attended the same school as the genie, granting three wishes.

The Three Little Pigs matched wits with a big bad wolf who also knew the power of three, declaring that he would do three things: "I'll huff, and I'll puff, and I'll blow your house in." He didn't include "and then I'm going to eat you," because that would have thrown off the rhythmic flow and was probably a given anyway.

Before crossing the street, we are taught to stop, look and listen. On the day that the firefighter comes to our school, we are taught to stop, drop, and roll. We are wired to remember things more easily when they come in threes.

No less than Solomon himself offered the phrase. "Eat, drink and be merry." The Declaration of Independence grants us the right to "Life, liberty, and the pursuit of happiness" here in the land of the Red, White and Blue. And isn't there romantic poetry in the pledge to "love, honor and obey"?

Having grown up with an inherent affinity for trilogies, the audience finds reassurance in stories and quotations that deliver the goods in threes. It took three ghosts to show Ebenezer Scrooge the error if his ways via visions of his past, present and future. Dorothy met up with three companions on her road trip to Oz, seeking a brain, a heart, and courage. The Three Stooges were a virtual three ring circus unto themselves.

Joke writers know the power of three and use it to great advantage. Not only does the power of three provide the rhythm of classic setups like "A banker, a lawyer and a politician go into a bar...", but the punchline is sometimes delivered third in a series. ("Marriage has a ring to it: an engagement ring, a wedding ring, and suffering.")

The very storytelling structure we rely on of *beginning, middle* and *end* even owes a debt to the rule of three. We consciously build stories with the basic formula of 1) setting it up, 2) telling the story, and 3) wrapping it up.

There are, of course, other numbers that made their mark in literature and lingo, like the seven dwarfs or the Twelve Days of Christmas. One could bring up the nineteen rings in *Lord of the Rings*, but technically the elves were allotted *three*, so there ya go.

There's just something magical about the number three. It's an easy number to work with, and much like the three doors contestants have to choose from on *Let's Make a Deal*, it's more interesting than two and less confusing than four. Use its power however you see fit, inspired by its ability to add a little extra magic to the story you put your blood, sweat and tears into.

MAGIC MINUTES AND FORTUNE COOKIE PROTOCOL

While we're discussing things of a magical nature, I'd like to share this with you. When I get a hankering for General Tso's Chicken, some good friends often go out for Chinese with me. At the beginning of our friendship years ago, I was a little taken aback by a ritual they perform when it's time to open the fortune cookies. They contend that each person must be handed their cookie by someone else at the table. So each person delivers a cookie as well as receives a cookie, all decided upon randomly. Ideally you don't give a cookie to the same person who gave you one.

An odd custom, I've always thought, but I oblige. (This is in spite of the fact that everyone *knows* you must eat the cookie closest to you when the waiter sets them down, or else the fortune won't come true.)

On a similar note, I'm not sure where I picked up this idea over the years, but when you see 12:34 appear on the clock, you're supposed to make a wish during that "magic" minute. By the same token, another acquaintance feels the same way about 11:11. If we combined both theories we could be entitled to two wishes every day (four, if you work past midnight every night as I tend to).

Here's just one more for you (and there is a point to all this): A favorite couple of mine recently celebrated their sixth wedding anniversary. When I wished them a happy anniversary, the husband thanked me but said they don't celebrate it. Why not? He explained that instead, they celebrate the day they met, because thirteen years sounds more impressive than six. I said that was pathetic, and he said don't be talkin' trash.

I have yet to see a wish come true from a magic minute moment, and while Confucius sometimes hits the mark with a fortune, it's usually because it was generic enough to apply to anybody. (The one I once got that said, "You like Chinese food" would have impressed me had it said "You like General Tso's Chicken.")

So one might fairly ask, what's the point in harboring little traditions and superstitions like the above?

Deep down we crave a little magic. Even though we know it's whimsy, we would love to know the future and have our wishes be granted. We may not believe in genies or unicorns, but don't we all have a few eccentric beliefs we've created for ourselves, like wearing a lucky pair of socks on game day?

The little quirks people have are the very things that make people unique and interesting. When writing our stories, we can incorporate the things we observe or make up entirely new behaviors and beliefs to imbue our characters with and give them humanity.

The beauty of being a writer is that we have the power to create whatever reality we want, where anything we choose can happen. One doesn't have to write science fiction to create a story that's fantastic and where hopes and dreams come true. To a reader, that's a wish as good as granted.

Fantasy writer Terry Brooks said, "If you don't think there is magic in writing, you probably won't write anything magical."

You are indeed a magician. Believe in your magic pen and manifest whatever your fertile imagination can conjure up.

Just don't be talkin' trash.

WHAT IS YOUR READER'S TAKEAWAY?

While visiting with a group of friends, one of the fathers was telling us about an incident involving his neighbor's very large dog. The dog had come into his yard, and his two young sons (three and five) were playing with it. Things got out of hand and soon the dog had his three-year-old on the ground, pinning him down in what seemed a threatening manner.

Spotting this, my friend rushed to the scene and kicked the dog away, yelling words he doesn't normally engage in. (Don't worry, the child was fine, and, for that matter, so was the dog. The children started crying, however, more upset at their father's scary outburst than any perceived canine threat.)

After he told us this story, we would discover that each of us in our group had homed in on a different detail:

One of us was worried about the three-year-old (we all cared, of course, but we already knew the child was unharmed).

One of us wanted to scold people who let their dogs run loose.

One of us was shocked that our friend kicked a dog.

One of us was surprised that he swore in front of his little kids.

Me, I wondered what his wife had to say when she heard about all this.

What becomes evident in the telling of even a simple anecdote, is that each of us puts our own spin on anything we hear. Coming from different backgrounds and having agendas that are uniquely individual, we interpret things according to our personal filter.

Part of the fun of seeing movies with friends is that we all come away with different perspectives to share. One may point out ironic parallels in the arc of a secondary or tertiary character, while another may focus on foreshadowing that the rest of us missed.

Basically, each of us will always hear what speaks to us. Likewise, our readers will be selective in what they take away from our writing. They may literally read into it things you didn't even write! As communicators with a story or a message to convey, we stand the best chance of reaching everyone on their level by presenting our ideas with enough clarity that they discourage misinterpretation.

Welcome—even celebrate—the many and varied trains of thought your words are likely to trigger. As long as your main points hit the bull's eye, that's as good as any communicator can ask for.

RIGHT BRAIN WRITING

SECTION V

BRANDING AND PROMOTION

Chapter 12
THE TITLE

"When you find the perfect title, the entire project seems to just fall in line beneath it . . . when you get the title right, it's a better feeling than finishing a book."

Richard Rushfield

IN SEARCH OF A TITLE

Companies spend millions of dollars in research and development to name their new products. For authors, a book title is a marketing decision that has a powerful effect on their "brand". A good title won't guarantee that a book will do well, but a bad title can surely decrease its chances.

Choosing the perfect title for a book can be as agonizing for an author as how to start the first paragraph. With an infinite pool of possibilities, how can you narrow it down to the most fitting, most irresistible title?

As always, it helps to take a cue from the pros. In reviewing recent bestsellers, most of the titles fall into one of four categories:

Simple Nouns
Descriptive Nouns
Situations
Statements

Let's look at a few:

Simple Nouns
A single evocative noun or nouns, conjuring curiosity.

Partholon by D. Krauss
Dollface by Renee Rosen
The Scroll by Miriam Feinberg Vamosh
Wink by Eric Trant
Moonrise by Cassandra King
Shattered by Rita Schulte
Sick & Tired by Kimberly Rae
Unseen by Karin Slaughter

Descriptive Nouns
Getting more specific, narrowing in on a particular subject.

Little Tea by Claire Fullerton
Song of the Meadowlark by Sherri Wilson Johnson
The Midnight Library by Matt Haig
Starry Night by Debbie Macomber
The Wishing Well Curse by Lynn Donovan
The Tempest Murders by p.m. terrell
The Gentleman Poet by Kathryn Johnson
Two Little Girls in a Wading Pool by Sara M. Robinson
Relative Danger by June Shaw
Tinseltown Riff by Shelly Frome
Glimpses of Glory by Peggy A. Keady
The Preacher by Michael Hicks Thompson

Situations
Identifying the central premise in the story.

Murder on the Orient Espresso by Sandra Balzo
Breach of Power by Chuck Barrett
Falling for the Lawman by Ruth Logan Herne

Taming the Sheriff by Cynthia Hickey
Being Santa Claus by Sal Lizard
Murder at Castle Rock by Anne Marie Stoddard
Love on the Brain by Ali Hazelood
Last Chance for Justice by Kathy Macias
Looking for Me by Beth Hoffman
Death of a Dowager by Joanna Campbell Slan

Statements
A complete sentence alluding to the idea behind the book.

Mama Was the Queen of Christmas by Linda J. Gilden
Mama Was Trashed by Deborah Sharp
I'm Glad My Mom Died by Jennette McCurdy
Murder Has Consequences by Giacomo Giammatteo
It Ends with Us by Colleen Hoover
Nothing Gold Can Stay by Ron Rash
Sometimes a Light Surprises by Jamie Langston Turner
March with Me by Rosalie T. Turner
Who's Your Daddy, Baby? by Lisa Pell

So, which seems to be the most common choice? Scanning the latest releases of 500 authors, the percentage of those title categories breaks down thusly:

Simple Nouns = 13%
Descriptive Nouns = 44%
Situations = 35%
Statements = 8%

At 44%, nearly half of the titles are descriptive nouns, identifying the subject of the book up front. That's not to suggest that one choice is better than another, but it may be a trend to consider if your current work-in-progress has a unique character, setting, or issue you can capitalize on when giving your story a novel title.

HOW TO PICK A CLASSIC TITLE

Every author wants a book that will hold its own against the 300,000 new books that are published in the U.S. each year. To give it a fighting chance, it has to capture the reader's interest instantly with a solid title that makes the right first impression.

Again, we learn much from the ones who've gone before. Let's break it down further and see how some of the classics of literature did it:

The Main Character
Dracula
Jane Eyre
Moby Dick
The Great Gatsby

What could be easier than simply naming your book after its lead character? That said, don't do it. These books were written in a different era, when it was in vogue to do so. *Robinson Crusoe* and *Anne of Green Gables* sound classic to us today because they *are* classic. In this day and time, it's highly unlikely that a new release called *Mrs Thornbush* or *The Adventures of Wallace Hampton* would attract anyone's attention.

If you must pay homage to the hero, these days it's more popular to keep things faceless and generic, like the titles of these New York Times bestsellers:

The Girl on the Train
The Murderer's Daughter
The Water Dancer
Diary of a Wimpy Kid

The Setting
Where the Crawdads Sing
All Quiet on the Western Front
Little House on the Prairie
Treasure Island

This approach, immediately answering the question of "Where?" still works as long as the locale happens to be intriguing or evocative like in the above examples or, in more recent years, *The Great Zoo of China*. John Grisham's *Gray Mountain* and *Sycamore Row* say little as titles, but hey, he's John Grisham, and it's his name that sells the books.

Overall, it's better to play it safe with some of the following titling strategies:

An Inkling of the Premise
The Call of the Wild
Kidnapped
Little Women
The Scarlet Letter

Giving your reader insight into the subject matter gets their imagination going.

Or perhaps you'd like to get specific:

Literal
Around the World in Eighty Days
Journey to the Center of the Earth
The Time Machine
Mrs Harris Goes to Paris

Identifying the main premise simply and directly may help your reader determine instantly that it's something of interest to them.

Intriguing
Lord of the Flies
One Flew Over the Cuckoo's Nest
The Color Purple
Cat on a Hot Tin Roof

Would you have any idea what these books were about from the title alone? Unlikely, but their vague insinuation of significance conjures curiosity. As with more recent bestsellers like *Go Set a Watchman* and *Secondhand Souls*, a thought-provoking title demands extra consideration.

And then there are titles whose very wording suggests an air of greatness:

Poetic
For Whom the Bell Tolls
Gone with the Wind
The Grapes of Wrath
Of Mice and Men

Again, the premise is unclear, but the overall feel of erudition imbues it with a sense of dignity. *All the Light We Cannot See* is a more recent example. You feel smarter just saying it.

Evocative
Kill Me If You Can
A Dance with Dragons
A Trick of the Light
The Language of Flowers
Flash and Bones

All of those titles pop, and even the most indistinct of them bear some connection to what lies between the covers. In all cases, if the title doesn't say it all, the supportive artwork fills in the gap.

Whether it's your book, movie, blog, or YouTube video, it never hurts to declare your intentions with a solid title. You can still get creative as long as you decide on a name that evokes some idea of what you're going to deliver. Whichever the case, you'll want to avoid a title that's too plain, which could cause you to be written off, having evoked no reaction at all.

Choosing the right title for your novel is one of the most important things you'll do, but it needn't be the hardest. Find the title that is an inviting reflection of what makes your book unique, and you'll have your reader at hello.

Chapter 13
THE COVER

"Good cover design is not only about beauty... it's a visual sales pitch. It's your first contact with a potential reader. Your cover only has around 3 seconds to catch a browsing reader's attention. You want to stand out and make them pause and consider, and read the synopsis."

Eeva Lancaster, author and book designer

RUNNING FOR COVER

You may have heard about a new research study that made this stunning discovery:

Women who wear makeup appear more professional.

Really? Who would have guessed such a thing? That study seems about as necessary as the one that explored whether men who wear ties look more authoritative. I'm seriously considering applying for a grant to see if being given a million dollars enhances your bank account.

Some things are just so obvious that it's hardly worth the thought. And yet—going back to the makeup thing—it's surprising how many authors overlook the importance of putting on a good face; that is, giving their book an attractive cover.

We've talked about making a strong first impression with an intriguing title. The other essential key to wooing a potential reader is using the look of the book to hook.

Granted, if you've been lucky enough for a major publishing company to accept your manuscript, they're going to commission the artwork and layout themselves. In that scenario, the publisher takes care of the creative post-production. A writer need only conjure up a great book and, after publication, look presentable at book signings (lipstick optional, although apparently highly recommended).

Meanwhile, in this modern era of self-publishing, more and more writers assume complete control over the entire process, including designing their own cover, with varying results. To their credit, some self-published books look remarkably professional, easily on a par with the bestsellers they share shelves with. Regrettably, many others don't do justice to the excellent words inside. Sometimes you can't even read the title because of the wrong font or color choice.

A poorly shot photograph or indistinct design screams "amateur", and a potential reader will automatically assume that the book itself is equally out of focus. Likewise, a friend who does some painting on the side may not be the best choice to help you put your best foot forward. The price will be right, but you'll pay a higher price when book sales disappoint.

Those who've already been there recommend seeking out an artist or photography pro, perhaps one near you, whose style resonates with you. They can easily be found online, where you'll see examples of their work. Stock photo sites are also ideal for scouting out images. In conjunction with the artwork, someone with a trained eye for graphic design can be enlisted to put it all together in an attractive format.

Then, just as you've gotten some trusted, literary-minded acquaintances to read your manuscript and give you practical feedback, don't skimp on seeking qualified judgment on your proposed cover graphics. Artistic opinion is especially subjective, so get as many critiques as it takes to be sure you've got yourself a winner.

Keep in mind that your book cover will often first show up as a smaller thumbnail on Amazon and other book sites. That thumbnail should be readable and eye-catching enough to compete with the other titles surrounding it.

What if your book is already on the market and you realize your cover is not what it could be? Don't kick yourself. Some of our favorite self-published authors have changed their covers in recent months, using their second-edition printing to upgrade. They report that the investment is paying off.

You've poured your heart into your book. Why not get it in the hands of your audience by making it one they'll be proud to be seen reading in public, and inspires others to ask, "What's that your reading?"

THE COLOR OF YOUR COVER

Remember what a magical experience it was to get your first big box of Crayola crayons, in "64 different brilliant colors"? You may recall having favorite colors and scorning certain others. I myself was never fond of periwinkle. It just seemed like a tepid, anemic shade of purple.

From childhood onward, colors elicit emotions that affect our mood, appetite, and purchases. Advertisers use this to great advantage, and it's to our own advantage to recognize how important our color choices are when it comes to designing book covers.

Consider the following color schemes. You know right away what kind of story you're in for, as each of these is an evocative reflection of their genre.

Someone's Gonna Die

Colors being able to speak volumes is probably never more apparent than in the mystery / thriller category, where darkness rules and the color of crimson drips freely, as in the stark black and red covers of suspense authors such as Amanda Kyle Williams, Steve Bradshaw and Robin Perini. Dr Richard L. Mabry takes a slightly different but equally effective approach, adding white to suggest a sterile forensic environment.

Don't Be Too Afraid

Contrast those dark and stormy covers with the colorful whimsy of the cozy mystery. Tonya Kappes, Peggy Webb and

Fran Stewart are among those whose covers let you know up front that murder can be fun too. Bright primary colors abound in quaint scenes that assure you it's all gonna be okay.

That's Amore

Red isn't just for Valentine's Day. The lush and sometimes passionate covers of romance authors like Kellie Coates Gilbert, Julie Lessman, Joshilyn Jackson and Tamera Alexander will make you see red, along with an abundance of pink and purple, other popular hues that harken the heart.

Moody Blues (and Browns)

Faded sepia tones remind one of an old photograph and suggest the past, as in *This Side of the River* by Jeffrey Stayton. The shadowy almost-gray of Ernie Lindsey's *War Child: Judas* suggests the turmoil of its dystopian setting. The muted tones of Linda Viden Phillips' *Crazy* reflect the cloudy mind of its protagonist. The cold gray-blue of Merle Temple's *A Ghostly Shade of Pale* creates a mood of the chilling danger ahead.

It's Beginning to Look a Lot Like Christmas

Traditional holiday colors of red and green, with bonuses of snow white, silver and gold, help to make the season bright. Holiday releases like those from Ann H. Gabhart, Fern Michaels, and Kathy Macias leave no question that Santa Claus is coming to town.

There are exceptions to every rule, of course, and plenty of successful books have bucked the tide and went against stereotype. But a good starting point when planning your cover is to see if the parameters of proven palettes will reinforce the mood of your project.

WHAT'S YOUR TYPE?

One font meets another font in Rome. He asks, "Are you a

Roman too?"

"No," says the other, "but I am an Italic."

If you understood that joke, you've come to the right place. You're a font-savvy scribe who pays attention to the typeface you use, and you prefer some over others. You don't have to have a font obsession like TV's Brick Heck (*The Middle*) or Sheldon Cooper (*Big Bang Theory*) to recognize that some typestyles work better than others, depending on the project.

For most of our writing, the default fonts do the trick just fine. Arial or Times New Roman are familiar friends and easy on the eyes. But there are times when you want something that isn't so ordinary, say, for a book cover or an author website.

For the sake of simplicity, let's narrow down all fonts to one of three types: **Serif**, **Sans Serif**, and **Decorative**.

Serif fonts like Times New Roman, Minion Pro, and Garamond contain hooks, feet and other embellishments. Studies have shown that Serif is the easiest type of font to read, which is why almost every book from the beginning of time has used it. This classic font is ideal for long stretches of copy.

Sans Serif fonts like Arial, minus all the ornamentation, are simpler and considered by some to be a bit more modern. A Sans Serif has a clean look that advertisers and signage of all kinds have relied on for decades. The Sans Serif font Helvetica is so popular that it was the subject of a 2007 documentary.

Decorative fonts have personality and, used sparingly, are good at establishing a mood. They are only to be used for titles and headlines, *never* for body text. A little goes a long way, and if there is too much of it, the eye fatigues quickly. If you've ever visited a website where all of the body text is in a decorative script, you know how painful it can be.

A look at the covers on a typical New York Times Best Sellers list shows no preference for either Serif or Sans Serif fonts. Both are used almost equally for titles and author identification. Decorative fonts are much rarer, appearing less than 10% of the time. In almost every case, the background or foreground art gets center stage, while the text is merely complementary.

These two book covers are simple examples of how font choice can make or break a design.

The tasteful one on the left can be read even from a distance using bold text and good color contrast, and its tall font is a good match for the tall shape of a book. You could say it hits the bulls-eye.

Where do I begin with the one on the right? First of all, it's a decorative font that wasn't designed to be in all caps, nor do the two ornate fonts play nice together on the same cover. Along with leaving hardly any border on one side, the font is barely discernable against the busy background.

In the end, it's all about communication. Feel free to experiment with style to get attention, but only take it as far as you need to. You'll never want to sacrifice clarity for creativity.

Chapter 14
SELF-PROMOTION

"Learn self-promotion. Share your vision without coming across as 'salesy.' Don't be afraid to ask for the sale, and always client focus."

Timi Nadela

HOW TO MAKE PEOPLE WANT TO READ YOUR BOOK

Perhaps the most valuable lesson in advertising and sales is the realization that nobody *wants* to spend money. However, they can be *persuaded* to spend it by a number of methods. The most time-tested way to do that is to make them believe that your product will change their life.

That sounds like a daunting challenge, if not an impossible task altogether, but in truth, it isn't necessary to change their entire existence, you merely have to suggest that you will improve it in some small way. The principle behind this is called "Don't sell soap, sell hope."

Let's go right to the source and see how they do it. Dove Soap knows better than to simply tell you their product will get you clean. They enhance the appeal with phrases like, "It's a refreshing, uplifting sensation for your skin." Irish Spring tells guys they'll get "healthy feeling skin the lasses can't keep their hands off" (which, appropriately, even slides a little Irish lingo into the equation).

Simply put, the buyer merely needs assurance that your product will enhance their life somehow. So how can you convince someone that reading your book or subscribing to your blog will change their life for the better? Ask yourself what the reader really wants.

If you write fiction, it would be easy to write off this analysis by declaring that they just want a good read, and since you've written a good read, end of story. On the surface, there's truth in that, but go deeper into the reader's dreams if you want to stand out from the 1.7 million other books that will be published this year.

Show them that your love story will transport them to an exotic locale where they'll get to experience the greatest romance they've ever known. Convince them that they'll share great adventures with your master detective and unlock the mysteries of life. Let them know there's a refreshing escape from the humdrum of daily life ahead for them if they'll just indulge in your book.

Do you write nonfiction? You'll find it even easier to target your reader's desires. They don't want to just learn how to use Excel, they want to become the recognized sultan of spreadsheets in their circle. Rather than merely learning the basics of home repair, they want to know they'll save hundreds of dollars and gain the adulation of their spouse next time the toilet backs up.

It isn't hard to communicate the implied promises of your book. A cover that conveys the right atmosphere can pull a reader in before the title even registers. Then the right title (and perhaps subtitle, if nonfiction) should reel them in. Beyond that, make sure your back cover and Amazon description convinces a potential reader that your book will provide an experience they cannot live without. Do that, and you've made a sale.

There are lots of reasons why people will want to buy your book. Zero in on those motivations by selling them hope—not soap—and you just might clean up.

HOW THE PROS MARKET TO TODAY'S AUDIENCE

Delicious! Refreshing! Exhilarating! Invigorating!

These enthusiastic adjectives were the sum and substance of the very first ad for a brand new product called Coca-Cola, circa

1886. The soda pop giant has been advertising as long as any other product that comes to mind, and, as always, it helps to take a lesson from the masters.

Mind you, it's not because we want to promote our books with over-the-top adjectives, but rather to observe how advertising experts like Coke have changed their strategies to adapt to the times.

Over the decades, Coca-Cola has been marketed by such monikers as "The Ideal Beverage for Discriminating People", "The Ideal Brain Tonic" and "The Drink of All the Year" (awkward as that sounds). It's hard to imagine these slogans having an effect on today's ad-weary and ad-wary audience.

As the buying public grew more sophisticated, it also became more skeptical, requiring proof to back up grandiose slogans. So ads went into considerable detail to fully explain a product and its particulars. "The bright tang of Coke is always welcome after a busy day of shopping. The bracing sparkle and the bit of quick energy you get in Coke makes it the perfect refreshment every time. It gives you a bright little lift; it brings you back so refreshed, so quickly..."

Compare that to more recent ads for Diet Coke. The primary message is that life is short and you should do whatever makes you feel good. (If that happens to be drinking Diet Coke, they wouldn't mind that a bit.) Rather than sell the product, they show attractive people enjoying it, hoping to entice consumers to follow their lead.

Today's buyer is more susceptible than ever to an invitation that makes them feel understood and important. In this age where they are bombarded with pop-up ads on PCs and video marketing at the gas pumps, they've learned to ignore blatant "buy me" marketing. Slice of life scenarios easy to relate to are what gets their attention.

That said, books are not soft drinks. Potential readers still want a detailed description of a novel to know what they're getting. But they are thirsty for a worthwhile experience, and buying books is a largely emotional and often impulsive decision easily influenced by the idea that something positive will come from it.

Would your book make a great gift for Father's Day? Graduation? Christmas? Somehow it feels like less of a sales pitch when the purchase will be an act of benevolence.

Will your book help the reader escape into a world of mystery, history, romance, chills? An evocative cover will do more to sell the sizzle than an aggressive come-on. Your website, blog and other marketing materials need be little more than a reinforcement of the experience the reader seeks to convince them that your books are exhilarating! Invigorating! Or—as Coke might say—the real thing.

Today, *soft sell* is king, and the advertising adage "Don't sell the steak, sell the sizzle" is as sound as ever. Especially if you can sell the sizzle with subtlety.

YOUR ADORING PUBLIC

During a memorable Johnny Carson interview, Jackie Gleason made a comment that serves as a reminder to anyone involved in the creative arts. The Great One and the King of Late Night were discussing what were the latest crop of '80s sitcoms and how they relied on canned laugh tracks. Gleason had this to say:

"We never did a show any other way but in front of an audience ... that's the only way to do a show. How are you gonna know if your timing [is right] if you haven't anyone to say it to?"

Standup comedians who have graduated from comedy club work to sitcom success will be the first to credit their on-stage experience as the school of hard knocks that helped them hone their craft. Honest, instantaneous feedback cannot be bought or learned in a textbook.

My many musician friends sing a similar tune about the difference between studio work and playing in front of a live crowd. While the perfectionist enjoys the luxury of recording and tweaking until they're satisfied, there is instant gratification and education that can only be experienced via an audience reacting to a live performance.

The ticket seller at my local movie theater told me about a little game she plays. Often, as a customer approaches the booth, she mentally tries to guess which movie they are coming to see. Parents with children, for example, are usually treating them to the latest Pixar flick. But sometimes she'll be surprised by a little old lady buying a ticket to see the latest action movie, or a not-so-young guy seeing *The Jungle Book* by himself (that would be me, by the way).

When the film studios get their box office receipts, they have no record of demographics to give them the ages, sexes, races, etc of those who came to see their movie. They can only gauge the success of their releases by how much they raked in that week. That is another advantage which connecting directly with an audience can give a TV star, a musician, and even a writer.

With endless avenues of media and entertainment available to today's audience, crossing over to try genres outside of their typical demographic is nothing new. Being aware of trends that interest your audience can be invaluable feedback that today's writer is wise to take into account. Especially when it's so easy.

Readers love to make any connection with their favorite author. A well-maintained website and/or blog is something they expect you to have. If your online presence consists only of an Amazon listing with no photo or bio, there is little reason or opportunity to try to tell you they enjoyed your latest book.

Social media may sound like too much of a challenge to those who've never tried it. But, when done right, it can be both an enjoyable and effective two-way tool for connecting with your audience. I recommend Edie Melson's *Connections: Social Media and Networking Techniques for Writers* to anyone intimidated by the idea of social media as well as anyone who's been doing it long enough that they have questions about content, frequency, etc.

Stephen King says he writes with a particular audience in

mind; an audience he is intimately familiar with. In his case, it's his wife Tabitha, who is his first reader. If you have a sense of who your audience is, and an awareness of what they like about what you do, you're in the best position to come up with what will keep them coming back.

WHAT BRAND ARE YOU?

Some years ago in a writing magazine, I noticed an advertisement for Kleenex®. But they weren't hawking facial tissue. This was a fairly official-looking admonishment to all writers advising them that Kleenex® is a registered trademark, and that whenever the word Kleenex® is used, it should be capitalized with the copyright symbol ® added to it.

Presumably this even mattered because people tend to call any brand of tissue Kleenex®, for example, "Could you pass me a Kleenex®?" You can already see how distracting it would be for writers to include the symbol in a novel. It's almost as distracting as the heavy-handed alternative, "Could you pass me a facial tissue?" People don't talk like that.

My gut reaction was that Kleenex® should just be happy to be such a frontrunner that they would become the go-to word for not just their product but all others like it. However, many products—from Ex-Lax® to Preparation H®—are equally, um, retentive when it comes to protecting their brand name.

It does have to be a little frustrating when you're Coca-Cola® and a substantial portion of the population refers to any kola nut-flavored carbonated drink as a "coke". But it feels a little over the top when a catchy TV jingle like "I am stuck on Band-Aids, 'cause Band-Aid's stuck on me" is changed to the clumsy "I am stuck on Band-Aid *brand*, 'cause Band-Aid's stuck on me". Awkwardly cramming "brand" in the middle of an established slogan sounded a little desperate.

You may be old enough to remember Funny Face Drink Mix (similar to Kool-Aid, with the kid-friendly flavors Goofy Grape, Injun Orange, Freckle Face Strawberry, Chinese Cherry, Loud

Mouth Lime, and Rootin' Tootin' Raspberry). In a short time, someone decided that two of the flavors were potentially offensive, so Injun Orange became *Jolly Olly* Orange, and Chinese Cherry became *Choo Choo* Cherry. (I'm surprised Rootin' Tootin' Raspberry wasn't vilified for being insensitive to cowboys.)

In more recent years, perhaps you noticed when the jingle "Ace is the place with the helpful hardware man" became "Ace is the place with the helpful hardware *folks*." (That one I do get, since a friend of mine's sister works at a hardware store.)

Clearly, companies go to a lot of trouble to protect their brand. If you're a writer, you have a brand that should be just as important to you.

While it may seem foreign to think of yourself as a product, consider Hollywood stars with established images, like Brad Pitt and Melissa McCarthy. It's hard to picture Pitt in a slapstick role, or McCarthy playing Anne Frank. Then there are chameleons like Jack Nicholson and Meryl Streep, who can do both comedy and drama, but then again, that very flexibility has become part of their brand.

The cover of any Stephen King book is distinctively Stephen King, evoking the bad vibes that lie inside. His Maine radio station WKIT is also fit for a King, with songs like "Black Magic Woman" and other ditties that would be right at home in a soundtrack to *Christine*. You know what you're gonna get when you buy a Stephen King book because of the consistency throughout his work and throughout his platform.

When readers see *your* name, what should come to mind? What image will help promote your books? Just what is it that you want to say to the world through your writing? These are good questions to ponder as you tweak your website and before you post things on Facebook. In defiance of the old saying, not all publicity is good publicity if it goes against the image you want to project.

As you go about developing your brand, follow in the attentive, consistent footsteps of proven marketing successes like Kleenex®. Becoming a brand people know and love is nothing to sneeze at.

STREET SMARTS

When a new shopping mall opened a couple of cities away from me, it attracted patrons from all over, as new malls tend to do. Ironically, no one in my circle has been there yet, and they all give the same reason: they don't want to fight the traffic. Indeed, the roads leading to and from this new mall were busy already, but now are said to be oppressively congested with regular traffic jams.

One of the town planners for my own burg says it's a classic case of putting the cart before the horse. Instead of planning for the future and widening the streets in anticipation of heavier traffic, those particular developers simply built the mall at a popular location, leaving the rest of the details to sort themselves out.

A *wise* planner leaves nothing to chance. An impact study would have dictated a more visionary sequence of events that would have accommodated both the mall's goals and its customers' convenience. Instead, the mall experiences as much negative word of mouth as it does positive.

Writers stand to benefit from strategic planning and implementation. The many steps in between first deciding to be a writer and vacationing in Monte Carlo to write your twentieth bestseller warrant an eye for detail and an ability to look down the road.

I'm not referring to the actual authoring of a book as much as what happens after that. As writers often ask, "I've written a book. Now what?" Here's a short list:

Website

When potential readers (not to mention agents and publishers) want to know who you are, they're going to look for your website. Not a Facebook page, but a website. Yes, have a

Facebook page too, but visitors want to see your photos, bio, book covers, and supporting materials all in one place on a website that bears your name. Don't wait until your book is on the market; the time to start publicizing yourself and your work is immediately, if not yesterday. Cash in on the free promotional tool that is the Internet.

If you're not ready to invest in a webmaster, take advantage of one of the free website hosts like Wordpress.com, Weebly.com or Wix.com to get you started. Their ready-made layouts in many categories offer drop and drag customization.

Press Kit

Basically, this is a tangible translation of your website that you can hand out. A well-done press kit says "pro" and is handy to have when you attend writers conferences or, of course, meet with anyone who can further your career. On a related note, be sure and send a press release to your local newspaper whenever your latest book is available.

Photos

Admittedly, some authors prefer to maintain visual anonymity, so this step may not apply. If it does, you will need at least one good photo for your website and press kit (next on the list). I mention this as its own entity to emphasize the importance of having a high quality head shot versus a selfie (although some cellphones do take amazingly good pictures). When you become the cover story of a magazine, you'll be asked for a high-res photo suitable for framing.

Proposal

If you're not planning on self-publishing and need to woo a publisher, one thing you'll want to use your time and talents for is creating a persuasive book proposal. How does one do that? Hybrid publishing acquisitions editor W. Terry Whalin's *Book Proposals That $ell: 21 Secrets to Speed Your Success* offers sage advice, especially for nonfiction proposals.

Book trailer

Every month, over two billion viewers watch videos on YouTube. If you've overlooked this enormous opportunity to get the word out, it's never too late to hop on the book trailer bandwagon. Some authors commission a slick presentation complete with narration, music and Hollywood-level footage; others very effectively just get on camera and talk about or read an excerpt from their book. A video trailer is a highly visible way to promote your latest release. It's also an ideal means to generate new interest in an older title.

The above list isn't all-inclusive, but successful writers consider these items must-haves for a writer's to-do list.

There will be over 1,700,000 new books published this year. Before yours hits the streets, avoid congestion and stand out in the crowd by creating a platform with a solid infrastructure. It will get you on the road less traveled.

PLAN AN EGO TRIP

It's ironic that authors who have no problem writing a 100,000-word manuscript on a deadline will freeze up when faced with writing their own author bio. Much like a resumé, the idea of encapsulating one's life and times into a few paragraphs is the stuff of anxiety and self-consciousness.

Whether it's for your Amazon author page or the "About the Author" section of your website, here are some time-tested tips to help you craft a credible characterization.

You is kind, you is smart, you is important

Taking a cue from *The Help*, come into the process with a positive self-image. This is the time to own what you've accomplished and to share it with pride. If you don't, who will?

Write in third person

Unless you're going for a friendly, folksy platform, it's

common practice to write your bio as an objective third party. Not only does it lend an air of endorsement, it gives you more liberty to tout your accomplishments without guilt.

Just like your novel, grab attention with the opening line

Instead of "John Q. Author has been writing novels since 2011," how about "After breaking both legs falling off a ladder in 2011, John Q. Author spent his recuperation time writing the first draft of his first novel." You can come up a creative first line without hurting yourself.

Tell it like it is

What are your interests and achievements that led you to writing what you write? Do you write science fiction because you once saw a UFO? Do you have a degree in medicine that propels your medical mysteries? Even a stint as a Walmart greeter is prime fodder if customers inspire your characters.

Note to fiction writers: If you have an interesting background, include that, even if it isn't related to writing. The fact that you spent five years living among apes may have nothing to do with your cozy mystery series, but it may make someone want to see what you've written.

Note to nonfiction writers: No need to get that personal. In this case, the reader mainly wants to know how they'll benefit from your work. Dwell on what they'll get out of it and why you're the best one to teach it to them.

In both cases, don't stray so far from your chosen genre that you confuse readers. If they seek you out as a historical romance writer, does it serve your purpose to say you collect DC action figures?

Which of these platform personalities do you want to project?

Jeff Goins, author of *The Art of Work*, says there are five basic personality types for author platforms. While this breakdown is designed for bloggers, it can help you pin down your bio personality as well.

The Journalist: Someone who seeks answers and asks questions of experts. By sharing those answers, they establish themselves as experts too.

The Prophet: A critic who feels things can be better and promotes solutions. This controversial role is not without its dangers, as everyone has an opinion and those who disagree can be alienated.

The Artist: Someone who creates art, music, photography, short stories, etc. and shares their work, perhaps even works-in-progress.

The Professor: Someone obsessed with details, data, and the way things work, taking complex things and breaking it down, usually with a takeaway.

The Star: Celebrities whose platforms are built on charisma or reputation. You may not think of yourself as a "star", but if people seek you out as the go-to person for your specialty, don't write yourself off too quickly.

One of these Jeff Goins categories may have spoken to you immediately; if not, you may be a combination, in which case you can morph them into an even more individualized persona.

Readers like to know who they're reading, so don't overlook this opportunity to let your little light shine via a bodacious bio. Take an ego trip, and pack your bags with confidence. You're not bragging if it's the truth.

LET THE SUNSHINE IN

Where were you during the 2017 eclipse? If you're like tens of millions of Americans, you went outside (or at least looked out the window) to try to catch your local version of the highly-publicized event.

Many who anticipated the solar show in the sky equipped themselves with cardboard glasses fitted with special lenses to protect their eyes. Others traveled to specific viewing locations with pricey black plastic eclipse goggles and a picnic lunch, enjoying their own little tailgate party. Some booked their hotel rooms months in advance to ensure their place in the path of totality, while others had no idea and wondered why it got dark outside for a couple of minutes. Apparently not everyone is blinded by science. (And hopefully nobody was.)

What makes this total eclipse a little more notable to any of us in the publicity game, is that this was the first eclipse where social media is to thank for really getting the word out. In the past, only the astronomers and devoted stargazers "saved the date" so far in advance. This time around, the buzz started very early via the Internet, and millions timed their vacations to be somewhere in the eclipse path on August 21st, 2017.

Social media is free advertising that works, but we already knew that. The real takeaway from this is that 1) the Internet buzz reached many who otherwise might not have cared and caused them to go to considerable effort in order to experience the event, and 2) the buzz began early enough that marketers, hoteliers, t-shirt manufacturers and commercial opportunists of all kinds could plan ahead and capitalize on it.

Publicity experts tell authors to start promoting their books months before they're actually available. One author I've worked with has been promoting her new August release since last Christmas, with excellent results. By the time it's released, the book will already be familiar in buyers' consciousness.

Posting progress reports on Facebook ("Just finished chapter 20!") or posting small samples online are simple ways to attract early attention. Some authors do contests, offering to name a character after the winner. Others ask readers to vote for their favorite of several proposed titles or covers. Getting fans involved makes them feel personally invested.

Generating buzz well in advance of your book's release and positioning it as an "event" is an easy but powerful strategy for attracting new readers and building their anticipation. Like a good solar eclipse, a successful book launch doesn't just happen. You planet.

SPEAK EASY

In every successful writer's life, it's likely the time will come when you speak in front of an audience. Perhaps a writers' group will approach you to be a guest, or you yourself will seek out a suitable venue to promote your book. In either case, few authors are trained in both writing *and* public speaking, so first timers sometimes learn the ropes the hard way.

Recently, I had the opportunity to attend a talk by a physician whose latest book had just been published. The newspaper blurb indicated that he would be discussing his book, and since the subject matter was of interest, I did indeed check it out. During that hour I was reminded of certain presentation do's and don'ts that I need to remember and which I hope will benefit you, too.

"And now a man who needs no introduction"

More than one comedian has introduced someone with those very words and then walked off the stage. Most of us, however, want and need to be introduced to the audience. Do yourself a favor and come up with the wording you prefer. Provide the person introducing you with a short paragraph about you. This info may already be in the program if there is one. Only if you're good friends with the presenter would you want them to adlib an intro for you.

Testing, one, two, three...

Whenever possible, check the sound system personally beforehand. At the weekend talk I attended, the author no sooner started speaking when deafening feedback filled the room. A sound guy rushed to his aid and quickly adjusted something, but at least four more times during the talk additional screeches marred the presentation. To the author's credit, he waited patiently each time and never called attention to it, much less made any disparaging remarks.

You Ought to Be in Pictures

Not every talk needs a slide show or PowerPoint presentation, but if you're going to have one, make sure your laptop is plugged in. A few minutes into his program, the author's slides were obscured by a popup message about the battery getting ready to die. The next few minutes were devoted to someone retrieving a power cord and eventually restoring the visual aids. Fortunately, the audience took it in stride and even saw the humor in it, aided by the author's own willingness to joke about his error.

Me, Myself and I

Technical problems aside, something the author could have done better involved the subject matter of the presentation itself. The audience came expecting to hear wisdom based on his new nonfiction book. Instead, all we learned was where he grew up, where he went to school, and how he got into medicine, accompanied by photos of all the people who encouraged him to become a doctor. It's one thing to share one's background, but the introduction could have covered the essence of it more succinctly.

To our disappointment, the book itself was mentioned only a couple of times, and when it was, just one helpful bit of info was shared. Yes, we got to know the author, but we didn't get to assess whether his book would be worth having. Bottom line: deliver what the audience expects.

See how the pros do it

Watch some videos of talks given by leading authors and observe how their presentations reflect their brand. Your favorite authors are readily found on YouTube. I'll recommend this one by Amalie Jahn, which I return to periodically. Her TED presentation is a prime example of poise, humor and information. You'll find it here:

http://www.amaliejahn.com/blog/chapter-23-ted-talk-me-on-the-big-red-dot

Presentations don't have to be flashy or slick, and you don't have to be the great orator. Just being yourself and giving the audience something they can take away, whether it's useful instruction or a heartfelt story, is what will make your talk one they'll appreciate.

ENJOY THE SILENCE

A public speaker who I had the pleasure of seeing recently—a competent and well-spoken fellow—began his presentation by declaring that he's probably going to talk too fast and talk too much. He went on to explain that he cannot bear to hear any silence during his presentations. The quiet moment between sentences makes him uneasy and he feels he must fill the gap with words. As a former radio DJ, I totally understand the dread surrounding "dead air".

We've talked about pacing as it relates to storytelling, and how important it is to provide readers with a roller coaster ride that takes them to great heights and then pauses momentarily, giving them a chance to catch their breath. But it's easy to forget that the principle of ebb and flow is equally important when addressing an audience.

Standing at the podium, a roomful of silent people is indeed very unnatural, especially with all eyes on you. Hoping as we are to regale the crowd, any silence feels like a vacuum. But if we flip that scenario and instead are seated in the audience, we can actually be quite appreciative of those pauses, which afford us the opportunity to absorb the information we're taking in. (Especially if we're trying to take notes.)

A good rule of thumb might be this: Any time you make a

statement that you consider deep, important, or potentially confusing, make a point to take a long breath while it sinks in. Join your audience in enjoying the silence. As long as you don't look like you're fumbling for the next thing to say, the audience will comfortably follow along at your pace.

Enthusiasm is infectious. Authors who regularly speak at conferences know that if we have a passion for what we're talking about and a genuine desire to share it with others, it will be hard to fail in front of an audience. With that in mind, I would add that a fervent urge to talk about your pet subject is an additional reason we may talk too fast, or too much. Passion sometimes overthrows pacing. (But that's a topic for you romance authors.)

CASTING CALL

From time to time I like to watch a movie with the script in front of me. It's always fascinating to see the finished product alongside its original vision. One excellent and free resource site boasting a wealth of scripts from movies, TV shows, plays, musicals, and even radio dramas is www.simplyscripts.com. In the "Movie Scripts" section they provide links to everything from *Bridesmaids* to *Purple Rain* to *Strangers on a Train*.

If you're like most writers, when writing fiction you picture it all in your mind like a movie. And it's almost impossible not to form a mental picture of the characters, including the most momentary of bit players. Likewise, if you're writing nonfiction and actually know the people involved, their physical impressions are even more firmly entrenched.

Since we've been discussing self-promotion, let's combine elements of all of the above for this interesting scenario: Let's say they're making a movie of your life story, and you have to cast famous actors in the different roles. Who would you choose to portray you, your family, your friends, your workmates, and the other key players in your life, past and present?

It's not only a fun and entertaining exercise but a revealing look at your perceptions of those around you. You may even find that the hardest role of all to cast with any assurance of accuracy is yourself.

Most of us never will actually write down our life story for the world to see. But author Kimberly Rae says we all have a tale worth telling, if only to share with those who come after us. Kimberly speaks of her grandmother, who lived through the Great Depression and had to have a double wedding with her sister to save money. Because her rich legacy of adventures were never committed to paper, they can only be handed down through forgetful word of mouth until they eventually fade into oblivion. So Kimberly chooses not to let that happen.

By the way, don't think you have to be a celebrity to write your memoir. If nothing else, consider immortalizing the most significant events of your life. As Kimberly says, "Life is fragile. And beautiful. And each of us has experiences worth recording."

Will your story still be told a hundred years from now? If you write it down, the answer is yes.

SECTION VI

THE WRITING LIFE

Chapter 15
PRACTICAL CONSIDERATIONS

"If you want to make an easy job seem mighty hard, just keep putting off doing it."

Olin Miller

A MATTER OF TIME

Every so often, usually after the latest Marvel or DC Comics movie, someone will ask this question:

"If you were a superhero, what superpower would you have?"

Despite the many options one could envision, I'm rather proud to boast that my answer has stayed the same over the years. The reason I'm proud is because I think it's the most logical choice of all. My superpower would be the ability to stop time.

Imagine. If you could stop time in its tracks, you'd have all the other superheroes beat by a mile. You wouldn't need to leap tall buildings in a single bound (like Superman) because you could just walk. You wouldn't need super strength (like, say, the Hulk on a bad day) since you could simply go borrow a snowplow and push whatever's in your way. Everything—and everybody—would simply wait until you were done.

You may have come up with a superpower you think is better than mine, such as being able to go back in time and change the past. But come on, that could never happen. Let's keep it real.

In my scenario, deadlines wouldn't stress you out, since you'd have the power to stall them until tomorrow, or next month. Running late for a big event? Forget about it. Get there when you can, and stop for a sandwich on the way.

Seriously, marvel at this list of things you would accomplish: you'd have time to read every book and watch every movie you ever wanted to catch up on. You could write endless novels, learn new languages, become a master of any skill you desire. You wouldn't even need a cape.

You may be familiar with an Adam Sandler movie some years ago called *Click*, in which the hero was able to stop everything around him with a remote control. It was actually pretty entertaining. In fact, I wouldn't mind going and watching it right now. But I don't have the time.

Unfortunately, the closest most of us will ever come to stopping time is hitting *pause* on the DVD player. However, there are ways we can take charge of the hours we have.

Time management experts tell us to ask the "Lakein Question" (named after author Alan Lakein): "What is the best use of my time right now?" In other words, "Is this what I want or need to be doing right this minute?" If the answer is "no", you may be engaged in a waste of your time.

Separating the urgent from the important is the foundation of time management, and it's not always easy to tell them apart. All day long, our truly important tasks are interrupted by some urgent thing that can't wait—or *can* wait but we don't let it because it seems important—such as an email or a phone call. Meanwhile, the truly important item is relegated to the back burner again.

In their book *Time Management: Goal-Setting Guide to Create Time for Yourself and Your Business*, Chris Tracy and Brian Bailey recommend formulating an action plan consisting of short-term goals that lead to the accomplishment of your bigger, long-term goals. Having manageable goals that motivate you enough to see them through is a key to controlling your time instead of letting it take control of you.

Many authors give their goals precedence by committing to take part in NaNoWriMo, aka National Novel Writing Month. Can you write a 50,000-word novel in thirty days? Yes, you can, and writers who have even less time to devote to writing than you do have done it every November since 1999.

Break it down to 1,667 words (roughly seven pages) a day and it still amounts to a challenge, but that's part of the charm of National Novel Writing Month. It virtually forces you to write with wild abandon, focusing on reaching your daily goal instead of trying to make your first draft perfect. (When was the last time you wrote with wild abandon?) Plan on taking the leap this November and visit http://nanowrimo.org.

You may rightly be wondering, "Why is NaNoWriMo" in November?" According to writer and founder Chris Baty, the timing is "to more fully take advantage of the miserable weather."

But I hope you're also thinking, "Why wait till November?" Starting right now would have the additional benefit of finishing and eventually releasing your opus with different timing than the other 450,000 writers who will be plugging theirs soon after November.

Why not start today and give yourself your own 30-day challenge of 1,667 words a day? You'll feel like a superhero a month from now when you have 50,000 words under your utility belt.

IN PRAISE OF PROOFERS

We've all done it. We rewrite and revise and tweak to death until we're certain every word is perfect, only to spot a grievous error the minute we hit the Send button. Another set of eyes—preferably several sets—are absolutely vital for any serious writer. Have at least one experienced editor review your manuscript and ensure nothing gets overlooked. In the words of the prophet, check yourself before you wreck yourself.

A second opinion is vital for spotting problems or unclear passages in our writing. Knowing exactly what we intended to say, we ourselves may not pick up on things like:

Long stretches of dialogue that fail to reinforce who's saying what
Too many details that are irrelevant to the story
Too many accessory characters to keep up with
Names of characters that are similar, inviting confusion
Pet phrases or inside jokes that make the reader say, "Huh?"

There's also the whole issue of typos and improper punctuation. It's amazing how the same sentence can take on different meanings without properly placed punctuation. One of my favorite examples is:

A woman without her man is nothing.
A woman: without her, man is nothing.

Good editors and proofreaders are all about clarity. A missing comma here and an awkwardly worded phrase there are the kind of things they lose sleep over, because grammatical gaffes of any kind take away from cogent communication.

They might even question my use of the word "cogent" if "clear" would say the same thing with less bluster. "Bluster" might even be suspect. I'm grateful to my brother Ron, without whose proofreading prowess you would be reading a book with a lot more grandiloquence than I've subjected you to.

Many times in the editing process, classical rules clash and debates result, but whenever they do, the judgment must always be in favor of clarity; whatever conveys most accurately.

You know exactly what you meant to say, so you may not spot the impediments to communication that a good proofreader will notice. Don't skip that important insurance policy.

HAVE A BACKUP PLAN

I wore it like a badge of honor. The realization that I had gone five years without a computer crash was something to brag about, given the abuse I inflict upon my faithful PC every single day from sunup well into the wee hours. Thanks to reliable antivirus software and never clicking links I don't completely trust, my primary hard drive and three external portable drives had tirelessly processed thousands of writing, audio and video projects without complaint.

That all changed one day, when one of my Seagate external drives suddenly wasn't recognized by my computer. Noticing that it was very warm to the touch, I unplugged it and let it cool down. After 30 minutes it was good to go again, and it did fine for about two days. Then it ran hot again and I let it cool again. This sequence repeated about three times, until I plugged it back in and finally heard the clicks of doom.

My Seagate wasn't just getting overheated; the internal mechanism was now audibly failing, so I decided I'd better start archiving to DVD-R anything that hadn't yet been backed up on disc, which, in my aforementioned overconfidence, was considerable. Unfortunately, it was already too late, and no amount of unplugging and replugging would get it started again. I resigned myself to having to redo a lot of the work that was on there.

Then I remembered an old wives' tale about bringing a dead hard drive back to life by putting it in the freezer overnight. I figured, what have a I got to lose; I was already between a rock and a hard drive. So I wrapped it in plastic and put it next to the frozen waffles.

The next morning, I wasn't optimistic as I plugged it back in, until I heard the whirring of the motor and the computer ding that indicated recognition of the external drive. I was flabbergasted, not to mention elated. Supposedly, lowering the temperature affects the metal armature and unsticks it or something. But this was no time for speculation. Without delay I began to copy the most essential files to another drive, which worked great—for about 15 minutes, when my failing drive got hot again, and stopped.

Considering that the temperature made a difference, it occurred to me that perhaps all I would have to do was keep the hard drive cold and it would keep working. So I froze it again, but this time moved a small portable refrigerator into my office so the drive could sit inside and stay cool while I continued my archiving to disc.

Great in theory, but unfortunately a failure. Apparently, you can only do the freezer trick a limited number of times before the drive totally gives up the ghost. In every subsequent attempt, all I got from my frigid files was the cold shoulder.

I shared all those details with you in the hope that they may help you in a similar crisis, but the bigger lesson I wish to convey is that it's not only those web viruses everyone talks about that can waylay your computer. Hard drives and other components will eventually wear out. In that same month I talked to several other writers who had recently experienced hard drive crashes as well. There must have been something in the water.

One author friend lost a flash drive while on vacation. Some of its contents, luckily, were backed up elsewhere, but too much of it was gone forever. Another author who had just finished the first draft of her fourth novel barely had time to celebrate before her drive crashed. I can still feel the pain in her words, "I will never get those exact words back."

We all know people who've experienced this horror story. Perhaps even you. In fact, it's more likely that it *has* happened to you than it hasn't.

So, from one tortured artist to another, I encourage you to make sure anything you care about is saved to a disc or an extra hard drive (or via a backup "cloud" option, some of which are free) so you'll never have that sinking feeling of losing chapters you've written, family photos, or other priceless folders.

For the record, a refrigerator in the office has its benefits too.

GETTING AWAY FROM IT ALL

It's every writer's dream: Escaping to a private sanctuary where there are no distractions, perfect conditions, and all the time in the world to write the Great American Novel. I'm often reminded of a classic Dick Van Dyke episode in which he attempted just that, retreating to a cabin in the woods with his typewriter, only to end up doing everything but write. He adjusted his seating height endlessly, played with toy guns, and went for a world's record with a paddle ball.

Most of us identify with his failure to communicate. Even if we orchestrate the most ideal of circumstances, it's not a guarantee that inspiration will magically follow.

But take heart, because here are some of the many ways to reconnect with your muse so that wherever you sit down to write you won't be at a loss for words.

Retreats

Each year there are numerous retreats in idyllic locations designed specifically for writers. Looking at some that will be available this fall, for example, a farmhouse in Tuscany or a hamlet in Denmark could be just the getaway to get your literary juices flowing. With a price tag of a couple of thousand dollars, however, these retreats are clearly not in everyone's budget. But there's nothing to keep you from creating your own retreat in a favorite setting closer to home. Maybe a three-day weekend at a B&B would be just the right change of venue.

For a longer escape, you might consider the recent travel trend known as a silent retreat. Who wouldn't be able to write in a Waldenesque locale offering nothing but quietude? Well, besides Dick Van Dyke.

Conferences

There's a writers conference coming to a city near you soon, guaranteed. Whether it's a day-long intensive or a multi-day event, leaving the world behind to focus on the voices of experience is a push toward productivity.

Being in the company of other authors is a confidence-building bonus. Many conferences even include a writers' bookstore with discounts for attendees. By the end of the conference you'll be dying to get back to your keyboard to write.

Writers groups
Whether they meet once a month or more often, writers groups are an excellent way to stay committed to your craft as well as accountable. By design, no two groups are the same. Some focus on instruction and exercises, others resemble a support group or social club. Each has its own personality, which is a good thing, since you can evaluate them all and find the one that makes you the most motivated to write.

Staying in touch with other writers
The business side of publishing may be highly competitive, but it's always encouraging to see how non-competitive writers are with each other. We celebrate each other's success and are inspired by every new book release instead of envious. Welcoming one another like family, we readily share tricks of the trade. So it's easy to make friends in the writing community. Whether we foster those relationships through email, social media, or face to face, there are few things more stimulating than an inspired back-and-forth with another creative mind.

Some of my most invigorating conversations have been over lunch with writer companions. On a recent Thursday, four of us enjoyed a spirited repast at McAlister's Deli, and I came away with three really decent story ideas. I'm pretty sure it wasn't just the Kale Parmesan soup that triggered them.

Hanging out in an inspiring place
Where do you think best? What setting clears your head and opens your imagination? For some, it will be outdoors in a park. Others relax at a coffee shop. The library is a favorite hangout of writers, surrounded by all the literary masters. Museums and

art galleries offer a similar sense of communion with creative genius. Whether you plant yourself there with a laptop or stroll the halls contemplating something you'll write later, a brush with greatness never fails to inspire.

Wanderlust

Performing a routine task inherently causes your mind to wander, lusting for something more interesting to think about. You can use the thankless time spent washing the car or doing laundry to ponder a scene or a plot, unimpaired by the dull duty in front of you. Sort through story ideas while you're sorting socks and you could have the first paragraph of your next writing session ready to roll.

The Great Escape

When all is said and done, getting our words written is not a matter of escaping to a place of perfection. The most prolific authors say that where you write is not as important as getting in that chair and simply writing, period. Books get written through sheer will and the tenacity to see it through. So the real escape is sometimes from our own procrastination.

IN FRONT OF A LIVE AUDIENCE

In his Golden Globe acceptance speech for the movie *Django Unchained*, writer/director Quentin Tarantino provided some valuable insight into his approach to writing award-winners. Specifically thanking the friends who are part of his life when he is writing, he explained that they don't realize how important they are to the creative process.

"When I read it to you, I hear it through your ears," said Tarantino, who shares scenes with his friends, not so much to receive feedback as to test his work out loud in front of an actual audience.

We've all heard that it's good practice for writers to read their work aloud to see if it sounds as good in the ear as it does on the page. But wouldn't it be great to have a live audience to bounce every new scene off of?

Most of us actually do have that opportunity if we're connected to a writers group, as there are often fellow writers willing to stay late or meet separately for the purpose of some mutual critiquing.

At the same time, many of us are such perfectionists that we don't want to release our words until we ourselves have honed them to our personal satisfaction. Both methods do the trick, and it clearly depends on the individual. With as many approaches to writing as there are writers, it's all a matter of whatever works for you.

The question is, Is your particular approach working for you? Are you getting as much written as you'd like, and are you pleased with what's getting on the page? If the answer is no, perhaps another method would be worth a try.

If you're finding that you leave your critique group feeling confused or discouraged, it may be time to work as a loner until you regain your equilibrium. Or if you've written alone for so long that you find it hard to gauge how your adoring public will react, it could well be time to branch out and seek some hearing ears.

Whether we read our work aloud to ourselves or to others whose opinions we value, let's sing Quentin's Theme and hear our words through the audience's ears.

NOBODY'S PERECT

While we're on the subject, let's take some of the pressure off and recognize the beauty of imperfection.

What does it even mean to be perfect? If we refer to Merriam-Webster, we are pointed to such attributes as *flawless, accurate, pure,* and *absolute.* All are desirable characteristics in the pursuit of quality, but, as the saying goes, we are only human, and we all know how imperfect humans are.

The Starbucks logo is a subtle but effective example of how

imperfection is sometimes preferable. The original logo of the sea siren was perfectly symmetrical in every way. It was appealing—even kinda sexy—but at one point their marketing team determined she was too perfect, to the point of feeling plastic and unrelatable. So they made minor adjustments in her face and hair. The revised logo has barely detectable differences that make her subliminally more human.

Highly sought-after Navajo rugs contain discrepancies. You will find inconsistency in the patterns, shapes and lines. Some feel this is done intentionally to symbolize human imperfection. Others believe the flaws are not intended. What *is* intentional in both cases is the choice to not go back and fix them.

No two fingerprints are identical. Every snowflake has its own unique pattern. In some cases, it may require examination down to electron-microscopic levels, but it is decreed that no two things will be perfect duplicates of anything else.

My point is, we are not obligated to achieve perfection. Knowing this, we can write with greater abandon and cast aside fears of not attaining some unreachable standard. We can only do our best, and our best is all we ever need to ask of ourselves.

RIGHT BRAIN WRITING

Chapter 16
ACCENTUATE THE POSITIVE

"Keep your face always toward the sunshine - and shadows will fall behind you."

Walt Whitman

WHEN IN DOUBT

I often recall this Facebook exchange between two authors in my friends list:

Linda: There are days, like this one, when I want to shred my manuscript and throw my computer in the pond. It'll happen someday. I'll toss everything and take up basket weaving.
Kathleen: That just means you're a writer.
Linda: You mean other writers want to throw their computer in a pond?

This amusing dialogue (which I've been granted permission to share) was between authors Linda Yezak and Kathleen Y'Barbo. And each of these successful writers makes a good point:

1) You know you're a writer when you get frustrated with your writing.
2) Every writer gets frustrated with their writing.

Frustration and moments of doubt, however, don't stop Linda nor Kathleen. Around the time of that post, Linda Yezak's latest novel *The Final Ride* won First Place in Christian Fiction by the Texas Association of Authors. And Kathleen Y'Barbo's vast catalog would easily fill two shelves at Barnes & Noble.

Looking through the 33-million-plus book titles on Amazon, or reading the success stories of other writers, it would be easy to question our own value to the writing community. We sometimes forget that the struggles we face are the same ones shared by every writer.

"We learn from failure, not from success," said Bram Stoker. It is quite an achievement when we've honed our craft well enough to recognize when something doesn't meet our own standards. Especially something that we've written. The ability to distinguish the wheat from the chaff in our own writing is something most novices can't do, dazzled instead by the joy of simply getting words on a page.

A few months back, one of my favorite author/lecturers spoke to a crowd of fellow writers. She spoke openly of the insecurities she's had to overcome, including that of speaking in front of a live audience. If she had merely given a great talk (which she did), we'd have been impressed. But we respected her all the more because she shared her vulnerabilities. The entire audience immediately bonded to her as fellow victims of self-doubt.

It's nice to know we're not alone, and that even in frustrating moments we're honoring a grand tradition of all the writers who, like Stephen King, laughed in the face of rejection slips and even stuck them on a nail to impale them. Don't lose your battle for want of a nail.

Follow the advice of *Rise Up and Salute the Sun* author Suzy Kassem: "Doubt kills more dreams than failure ever will." Can that attitude help you succeed? Undoubtedly.

TRIPPING YOUR WAY TO SUCCESS

A good analogy might be Jennifer Lawrence at the 2013 Academy Awards. You may recall that the graceful beauty tripped on her gown while ascending the steps to accept her Oscar for Best Actress. A lesser thespian might have let the stumble spoil their acceptance speech, but the star of *Silver*

Linings Playbook laughed it off and went home with the gold.

The ability to "shake it off" is a prerequisite to success echoed in every field, from entertainment to sports to high finance. The pros know that the easiest way to hit a roadblock is to let a trip trip you up.

It is said that songwriters have to write a lot of bad songs before they can write a good one. That sentiment has been repeated so often by so many tunesmiths that it has become a cliché, and, like most clichés, it has its basis in truth. Of course, the same applies to any writing. We have to be willing to write a lot of bad paragraphs before we can inherently understand what makes a good one.

We learn more from our mistakes than we do from our successes. Going from good to great in whatever we do requires abandoning fear of failure and developing a willingness to take chances that take us out of our comfort zone.

Comedy icon Jerry Seinfeld recalls that he was "out of your mind nervous" the first time he appeared on Carson. Even now, decades later, he admits, "I'm very respectful of anyone who attempts to stand on that stage. It's a very difficult thing just to stand there." Yet he adds that it is that very discomfort that fuels him as a performer. "The worst thing is when you get comfortable. That's why success is the enemy of comedy."

Each week on TV we are treated to an endless array of workplace competition shows where standup comics, amateur chefs, tattoo artists and runway models are thrown new challenges and face possible elimination. The good news is, real life doesn't eliminate us when we mess up. The greater the error, the greater we stand to learn from it. In that spirit, we should feel a sense of accomplishment when we make mistakes that are epic.

One of the finest writers I know told me she was appalled when she re-read something she wrote a mere three months ago. Letting something sit and then visiting it with new eyes once the initial infatuation is over is one of a writer's most valuable experiences. Many successful authors have mastered the art of writing their first draft like a writer and revising the second draft like an editor.

As hockey legend Wayne Gretzky said, "You miss one hundred percent of the shots you don't take." In the creative arts, don't be afraid to challenge yourself beyond what you know. If you've fallen in love with writing, falling is part of the fun.

THE FACE OF FRUSTRATION

When we get frustrated, it helps to determine the real source of our discontent. Narrowing it down to the actual cause helps us to avoid red herrings and address the root of the problem.

I have less than fond memories of a coworker from years ago who was particularly abrasive. Nobody liked to see this salesperson coming, because whenever she approached, it meant she had a problem and demanded that you fix it. While she was not a superior, in my position at the time I was one of the main fixers, so I had no choice but to recreate a project, placate one of her difficult clients, or put out some kind of fire. Basically, her appearance at your door meant a terrible, horrible, no good, very bad day ahead.

Since she only darkened my door every couple of weeks or so, I managed to persevere for a few months before I decided something had to be done about it and analyzed the situation. Prior to this, I saw the problem as the extra work she created. But in truth, the work—while time-consuming—was not the real issue, since that was my job. What made it so unpleasant was the atmosphere caused by her high-maintenance personality. It made everyone around her uptight and fostered a negative, burdensome attitude toward the task ahead.

The work would still have to be done; no way around that. But my own attitude about it could change, especially if I could minimize the effect this person was able to have on me. Instead of allowing myself to feel put upon, I could attempt to defuse her demanding demeanor.

I managed to do that by responding to her next request not with the resigned congeniality I started out with, nor the "why are you always a problem" look it had developed into. Instead, I joked with her, made light of the situation, and handed her an invisible shovel for the early grave she was determined to send me to. Almost immediately her approach lightened, my attitude improved, and our future encounters of funny and friendly sparring actually turned into something we came to enjoy.

When we become frustrated with our writing, it's good to analyze the real cause and see what can be done to change that part of it. Stuck on a scene? Tell it to take a hike, write the next one, and come back to the trouble spot later with fresh eyes. Worrying about a looming deadline? Laugh in its face and start writing with a vengeance. Disappointed because your social media numbers aren't close to Stephen King's? Scoff at statistics and focus on quality followers, not quantity.

W.C. Fields called it taking the bull by the tail and facing the situation. It's not always easy to look trouble in the eye, but when we see the true face of frustration, we're better equipped to give the problem a kick in the pants.

THE THRILL IS GONE

After enjoying my favorite Chinese buffet this weekend, I cracked open my fortune cookie to reveal the following message inside:

Change is not just essential to life. It is life.

Uncannily, only minutes earlier, I had decided that I wanted to include some thoughts here about change. I don't know how Confucius does it.

What I do know is that I have heard multiple authors express the following sentiment: They talk about how passionate they are when they first come up with an idea and how passionate they remain during its writing, but once they finish the last page, something changes. The devotion that drove them is now replaced with a certain apathy. No longer do they feel an all-consuming desire to share their words with the world.

What is it that makes the passion go away? Possible culprits include:

Arriving at their destination. Their vision centered around getting the story out of their head and onto the written page. For many writers that's all they ever really asked of themselves.

Not wanting to take the next step. The fun part—the writing—is behind us. You mean now we have to find a market for it?

Fear of failure. Nobody likes rejection, especially after slaving over a hot keyboard creating their hard-fought masterpiece. If nobody ever sees it, then we're safe from criticism.

Fear of success. Seriously? Is that a thing? The idea that anyone would *resist* success sounds implausible, but we creatures of habit can be funny that way. Change is inherently scary, even when it's good.

There are many more passion killers, but you get the picture. When post-writing apathy creeps in and the thrill is gone, what can we do to change it?

We can remind ourselves that what we write has a purpose far beyond what we initially envision. Each of us has a message that is uniquely ours. When our muse compels us to write something, it should be our mission to make sure the world hears it. No one starts a writing project with a commitment that no one will ever see it (unless it's their diary).

We wouldn't be writers if we didn't have a voice that begs to be heard. When the writing is done, make seeing it through to its highest and best destination the part that's even more fun. The real thrill comes when your writing changes someone else's life. And someone is waiting to be changed by your words right now.

UNDERCOVER AT THE LIBRARY

Some time ago, while on business at my local library, I decided to investigate the fiction section to gather a little intel. Specifically, I was curious to see how many of the authors I've enjoyed some connection with were represented on the public shelves.

I started with the A's and was delighted by the appearance of Tamera Alexander, Christa Allan and Andy Andrews. Familiar friends Sandra Balzo and Nancy Cohen were not far behind. These authors and their publishers are among those who recognize the opportunity to reach new readers outside the bookstore by having their books placed in libraries.

By the time I got to the G's and spied Tricia Goyer, the silence of the library was broken when I detected the sound of live music being played. Making my way toward the event rooms to investigate, I came upon a woodwind quintet from the Memphis Symphony, entertaining about two dozen 5- to 12-year-olds through song and story.

The librarian would read a paragraph from a children's book and then the band would play, representing the scene that was just read. It was a clever and effective concept, combining reading with music, and I found myself just as enraptured as the small fry all sitting on the floor.

Occasionally a parent, themselves lured by the pipers, led their child into the room. One in particular caught my eye. This little girl, probably four years old, entered with a blank expression and her hands covering her ears. The music wasn't deafening so it was clearly to communicate her unfiltered displeasure.

I couldn't help wondering whether this tyke was raised on rap and considered melodies foreign and offensive, or perhaps she was more an aficionado of the cello and one wasn't present. None of this seemed to matter to the other 24 kids who hung on every note.

This library encounter provided a reminder of several things of value to this writer:

- Words and music each have a unique power to convey the entire range of human emotion. Put them together and you have an even more compelling experience. Authors who appreciate a well-scored motion picture often find it helpful to listen to music that fits the mood of whatever scene they're writing.
- Your audience will pay avid attention to you if they like what you're doing. (In some cases, they're willing to sit on the floor.)
- Whenever you do something creative, some critics are going to love it, while others simply won't. Keep in mind that it's always a reflection of them, rather than of you.

I didn't happen to notice whether the little girl ever warmed up to the presentation and eventually uncovered her ears. I hope she did and joined these other little lives that were enriched because somebody wrote good words and somebody else played pretty music.

Me, I still had big library fish to fry, authors to check out, and mysteries to solve. Like, who is Dewey and why do we still use his Decimal System?

THE RIGHT PERSPECTIVE

As we speak, virtual reality is gaining in popularity, especially with gamers. In movies, it's primarily science fiction and children's animated features that bank on the 3D fad. And we'll call it a fad until it's been around long enough to prove it doesn't wane again, as it has done after every past upsurge.

Moviegoers in 3D's early stages were subjected to a much cruder, early version of the technology we now enjoy with much greater clarity. Anyone who's ever worn the blocky, poorly-fitting cardboard glasses reminiscent of the 1950s remembers their ears getting uncomfortable long before their eyes, which suffered through the fatiguing task of interpreting blurred images of red and turquoise.

Most of those movies made for 3D were equally cheap and cheesy, written around special effects, lending themselves more to horror and comedy novelty throwaways than character-driven drama. *The Creature from the Black Lagoon* and *House of Wax* are among the few notable and enduring efforts. The Three Stooges even poked audience's eyes in 1953's *Spooks!*

But, much like Curly, 3D was a victim of circumstance. After a short three year run, the third dimension had pretty much run its course. By the time Alfred Hitchcock filmed a 3D mystery (*Dial M for Murder*), the awkward medium had met with its own demise, causing him to release the 1954 classic in regular 2D. One can only guess how Hitchcock would have used the effect to great advantage years later when he did *Vertigo*.

Today, 3D's highly superior incarnation tricks the brain with polarization rather than offset colors, yet it still only makes sense for certain types of features, like action movies or CGI animation that can take you places where real life (and cameras) cannot. It's highly unlikely there'll ever be a market for *Pride and Prejudice 3D*.

Lately, 3D TV is attempting again to make headway into our homes, now that we have the technology to take existing film and TV material and turn it into 3D. And with virtual reality coming, someday Ricky Ricardo could be singing "Babalú" in the middle of our living rooms. Be very afraid.

But for 3D to survive the next go-round, it must do more than fling gumballs at the audience; it has to immerse us into the story. And that still isn't done with visual trickery but rather with emotional depth. *Titanic*, while it has plenty of 3D action, also has enough plot and character to pull you in. It's movies like *Shark Night 3D* that are a mere novelty, though of course that's their intent, just like a dime-store novel meant for a quick read and an imminent future in the trash can.

As authors, it's easier to jump on the latest gimmick and come up with momentary fluff. Fortunately, most of us choose to put our efforts into crafting a book that will be deemed worthy of handing down to the next generation. If we can evoke genuine 3D feelings in the reader, they won't have to wear clumsy glasses to immerse themselves in what we write.

GETTING IN THE ZONE

Just a few weeks ago, the Mega Millions jackpot rose to over a billion dollars. Whenever the payout reaches such an astronomical figure, this question gets passed around:

"What would you do if you won the lottery?"

I find it encouraging that whenever writers are asked that question, among first words out of their mouths are, "I would *write!*" The luxury of having all the time in the world to indulge in their passion is every true writer's desire.

Certainly, paying off bills and traveling the globe get mentioned too, but the allure of writing to one's heart's content is the ready fantasy that gets a wordsmith's adrenaline pumping. The windfall itself is merely a means to an end, that of getting to live the writer's life to the full.

Wanting to do what we love is in our DNA. We have all experienced that blissful state known as being "in the zone." Everything is clicking, we're firing on all cylinders, and we lose ourselves in our creativity to the point where we're skipping meals and wondering how it got to be three in the morning.

Some call this equivalent of the runner's high "the flow state," because inspiration flows effortlessly. How fitting that the word *inspiration* literally means to be *filled with spirit*.

This heightened level of performance can be practiced and mastered using certain techniques, including these three time-tested methods:

Be present

Fully engage in what you're doing, moment by moment. Hopes and anticipation about the final outcome, while fine motivations, are only in the future. What you have control over is right now. Connect with the joy that is the journey.

Add a new element

A task that has become too familiar and routine invites boredom, so change things up. Approach each writing session by adding a new challenge that will stimulate growth. We are easily overwhelmed by too many new things at once, so just make it one small challenge at a time.

Eliminate negativity

Negativity is the enemy of creativity, says filmmaker David Lynch. Remove negative suggestions and influences, especially that worst crippler of all, self-doubt. Each creative session is a time for you to experiment free from fear and criticism.

Miles Davis had the right attitude, a mindset that helped him conjure the zone on cue. "I'm always thinking about creating. My future starts when I wake up every morning ... Every day I find something creative to do with my life."

The odds of winning the Mega Millions are an unlikely 1 in 302,575,350. But the achievable thrill of being in the zone can feel like winning the lottery. I want you to hit the jackpot every time you sit down to write.

EVERYTHING IN ITS TIME

There's a scene in *Back to the Future* in which Marty McFly dons a hazmat suit and tries to trick his father into thinking he's from outer space. To support the ruse, Marty uses his Walkman like a weapon to inflict hard rock on this 1950s fellow, whose musical awareness has only gotten as far as "Earth Angel." When the dad is introduced to heavy metal, he thinks his brain is melting. (I often feel that way too.)

It's a funny movie scene, but it evokes a stimulating consideration about the evolution of music as well as creativity in general. What would be Mozart's first impression if he was transported 200 years into the future and experienced a sudden dose of Iron Maiden? The possibility that his brain actually *could* melt aside, chances are he would interpret it as being so out of his realm of consciousness that it wasn't even a form of music.

Similarly, if we went back 1500 years and played Mozart to a group of medieval monks whose only exposure to music was vocal chants, they might well regard Wolfgang's complex concertos as the work of the devil.

As we watch the latest sci-fi summer blockbuster, one has to wonder how someone like George Washington would react if he walked into a 21st century IMAX theatre with a 64-channel Dolby sound system. The convincing CGI spectacles of planets exploding and warp speed travel through the stars would appear all too real and life-threatening, and another brain might melt.

We have progressed in mind-bending ways from the very first evidence of entertainment on the big screen, namely cave paintings. This art, created prior to the written word, is said to be a form of communication and that cavemen were the first storytellers.

Whether we're talking movies, music or writing, what we create today comes from a long and natural evolution of creativity. Jules Verne imagined a future that, in some respects, we have already surpassed. Dick Tracy's video wristwatch from the '50s took only a couple of generations to become reality.

What we imagine—and chronicle in any lifetime becomes an important stepping-stone in the future of mankind and culture. As writers, we play a vital role.

Marty McFly learned that each generation has its own voice, and that too much of a jump forward can be a jolt. Therefore, there's a lot to be said for all the parents who don't start their babies out on rock 'n roll, and instead buy their infants those "Classical Baby" CDs, said to give kids a smart start.

After all, we need to crawl before we can rock.

Chapter 17
DO IT NOW

"Tomorrow is not guaranteed. If it is worth dreaming about, it's worth fighting for now."

Rebecca K. Sampson

UNFINISHED BUSINESS

Having recently attended the funeral of a former professor, a writer friend was exhibiting a more philosophical side of himself than I usually get to see. His contemplations led us to the question:

If you knew you had only a year to live, how would you spend it?

I think most of us would share some of the same answers. We'd make sure our affairs were in order. We'd express our love and thanks to the people who've meant something to us. We may travel to some place we've always wanted to go.

These are things we would *do*. But I'd like to take that question a step further and ask:

What would you regret *not* doing?

Since you're a writer, you may be thinking of a particular book. Perhaps it's one you're working on right now. Or, just as likely, you may have an idea that's been nagging you for years. It won't let you forget it, even though you've kept it at arm's length for a number of reasons.

What is it about this book that causes you to keep it on the back burner? Is it too challenging, too honest, or likely to invoke criticism? Fair enough. But if it keeps haunting you, pay attention to that. It could just be that it's the most important book you're meant to write.

Herman Melville, Charles Dickens, Truman Capote, F. Scott Fitzgerald, Jane Austen, C.S. Lewis, and Mark Twain are just a few of the famous writers who had unfinished novels at the time of their death. Most of these books were published without endings. More recently, Stieg Larsson (*The Girl with the Dragon Tattoo*) left behind a string of synopses for future tales in his Millennium series, possibly to be written by his successor.

In his classic *A Year to Live*, Stephen Levine spells out the importance of valuing the nudges of inspiration we are given. Honoring them, embracing life more mindfully, and forging ahead fearlessly, we will be less prone to feel like our time has come too soon. Levine writes:

> "Last words are as spontaneous as the life that produces them. If we speak now with care and consideration, if we use our words now to express our heart, that is the voice that will speak for us as our awareness gathers to depart."

What are the words you want to leave behind? How will the world remember you as a writer, as a person? With the limited time we have to leave our mark, let's strive to do it with the truest voice we have to offer.

CARVED IN STONE

Several years ago, while visiting my cousin in North Carolina, I joined his family for an excursion to historic downtown Hendersonville, where their fine arts festival, Art on Main, was in full swing. We strolled the streets, encountering metal workers, portrait painters, authors, blacksmiths, and apple-flavored ice cream, though my favorite discovery was an enormous general store called Mast, a multi-story warehouse of curiosities which was like a Farmer's Almanac come to life. Their candy department alone was a treasure trove of forgotten and obscure confections.

Taking a break from our walking, we camped out on park benches next to a municipal building. As I toothfully worked on my first-ever Big Hunk (a taffy-like creation of honey-flavored nougat) I couldn't help but notice a concrete memorial right in front of me, honoring Vietnam veterans. It caught my eye because of its unique shape (that of the Vietnam coast itself) and also because of the wording carved at the bottom: "Designed by Jerry Gordon, 1947-1995".

I found it ironic that the person who used his skills to chisel this tribute to heroes has, in the process, likewise been immortalized. As a result, his name, too, will be seen in this spot for generations to come.

It brought to mind that you and I will someday leave behind a legacy of our own. The question is, what will that legacy be? As writers, we may hope it will be in the form of a bestseller that's still available fifty years from now.

The great authors who came before us are not only remembered via the printed page, but were found worthy of their own memorials. The homes of Emily Dickinson and Robert Frost are well-visited Gracelands in their own right. Walt Whitman and Kurt Vonnegut have libraries named after them. A statue of Mark Twain can be posed with, not just in his hometown of Hannibal, Missouri, but in other American cities as well as in Canada.

These beloved writers made themselves immortal by leaving a legacy of literature that captured the times as well as the hearts of their readers. The book you're working on right now may well become the masterpiece that defines this day and age to a generation to come. A lofty suggestion, perhaps, but it's unlikely that Nathaniel Hawthorne ever imagined that his likeness would grace the place he used to embrace.

Our literary efforts may or may not earn us a concrete memorial or a statue in our local park, but it's something to strive for. Next time you're thinking that writing is a monumental task, celebrate the fact that it actually could be.

GOING PLACES

I often accept the invitation to be a guest reader at elementary schools for Community Reader Day. Upon arriving, the teacher typically has a book already picked out for me to read to the kids. I'm surprised at how often the book of choice is Dr Seuss' *Oh, the Places You'll Go!*

It's always a pleasant surprise, since I enjoy revisiting this pint-sized pep talk by the good doctor, and the kids seem to get a lot out of it too.

I've been even more pleasantly surprised to learn that *Oh, the Places You'll Go!* is popular not just with grade school children, but is a perennial favorite of adults who give it as graduation gifts, wedding gifts, and to others embarking on any new path of life.

In this classic tale, the protagonist (you) gets to take a symbolic trip into your future, a land of unfamiliar trials and triumphs and ups and downs, always with the assurance that you will emerge the conquering hero. In the encouraging words of Dr Seuss, "And will you succeed? Yes! You will, indeed! 98 and 3/4 percent guaranteed!"

The most famous and powerful scene is one in which you come to a region called The Waiting Place, where everyone is just ... waiting. Waiting for the mail, or for Friday to come, or for a yes or a no, etc. In this city of stagnation, nothing ever happens because nobody takes action.

As we look back at our lives, how many of us can say that we haven't wasted time in that Waiting Place? Did we maintain a schedule of writing every day? Did we keep submissions going out? Did we stay connected through writers groups and conferences? Or did we put off our writing goals, waiting for conditions to be just right (which of course they never are)?

Following Dr Seuss's advice—if not that of our own personal compulsion—I can't think of a better prescription than to promise ourselves that we will not be victims of self-imposed inertia. Actions do speak louder than words, and when we combine action *with* words, great things happen.

WHAT WRITERS REGRET

One question often asked during interviews is, If you could change anything in your career, what would it be? Here is the answer most authors have given:

"I wish I'd started writing sooner."

This regret is echoed by writers of all ages, not just the ones who followed their inner Hemingway after retirement. The thrill of having publishing dreams come true at 25 is no less exciting at 75. But the bottom line is, no matter when they do it, writers regret not having started *sooner*.

What does this oft-repeated sentiment tell us? That authors who have experienced the joys and the struggles of committing to their craft have discovered it to be a rewarding enough undertaking that they only wish they could have had more of it in their lives.

Author Paolo Coelho wisely said, "One day you will wake up and there won't be any more time to do the things you've always wanted. Do it now." How deep will be the regret of would-be writers who always knew they had a book in them, but never even tried to write the first chapter?

For any of us who feel the urge to write, it's an essential part of our nature and something that will never be satisfied until it's fulfilled. Whether we put our everything into it now, or put it off for some distant future, the day will come when we say, "I wish I'd started writing sooner."

One thing's for certain. You will never say, "I wish I hadn't become a writer."

A WRITER'S BUCKET LIST

The term "bucket list" has become so much a part of our lexicon that it's hard to believe it wasn't a common phrase prior to the 2007 movie *The Bucket List*, starring Jack Nicholson and Morgan Freeman. In a short time, most everyone came to know that a bucket list is a personal wish list of things one wishes to do before one "kicks the bucket."

No doubt the phrase caught on so quickly and indelibly because everyone has their own deeply personal wish list, regardless of whether they've taken the time to write theirs out or not.

Examples from the film include "Witness something truly majestic" and "Laugh until I cry". Goals like these are not mere short-term achievements like clearing out your inbox. They aspire to the kind of high-caliber life experience that fulfills on a soul level.

As a writer, it's a given that some of the goals capable of enriching us to that degree will involve writing. Why not include something "bucket list worthy" in your intentions?

Where to begin? A good place to start might be asking yourself the main questions posed in the movie:

Did you find joy in your life?

Has your life brought joy to others?

When we narrow these into a writing focus, they might well become:

What will bring me joy in my writing?

How can my writing bring joy to others?

A good bucket list item reflects the motivation behind it. Instead of "Write a novel", make it "Write a novel that honors my ancestors" or "Write a book that helps kids who are afraid of going to the doctor". One of the best things about a bucket list is that it's uniquely you, and exclusively yours to fulfill.

May you write something capable of changing someone's life, and your own. You might even come up with a new catch phrase, like "bucket list".

THE MONTY HALL PROBLEM

To clarify things right off the bat, Monty Hall himself is not a problem. The original host of *Let's Make a Deal* led a good life and remains an inspiration to his fellow game show hosts.

"The Monty Hall Problem", on the other hand, is a thing, and one that's been debated for decades. It is a brain teaser having to do with probability, one which has puzzled great mathematical minds and caused university professors to write papers on it.

As you may know, the biggest deal on Monty's game show would involve three doors, behind one of which would be an awesome prize like a brand new car or a European vacation. Behind the other two were far lesser prizes, one of which would be a "zonk" like a goat or a lemonade stand. To play the game, the contestant would choose a door, and Monty revealed what was behind one of the doors not chosen. Then Monty would give the contestant a chance to change their mind about which of the two remaining doors they want.

This is where the debate comes in. With three doors, it's clear that the contestant has a 1-in-3 chance of winning the big prize. After one door is revealed, has the contestant's odds of winning improved? Is it still a 1-in-3 chance or has anything changed that? I have my theory, but I'll let you mull it over first, or even go Google "The Monty Hall Problem" if you really want to boggle your brain.

Writers today have a similar gamble to make. When we invest ourselves in writing a book, we don't know what the outcome will be. Will it get picked up? Will it sell? Will it end up in a yard sale? We could further complicate the equation with additional options like, should we self-publish or go traditional? We could create any number of mystery doors for this analogy.

What it really comes down to is this question: What would it take to make us feel like a winner? For some, it will be the simple pleasure of having finished the book we always intended to write, whether it makes it to print or not. Others dream of opening that box filled with copies of their shiny new book.

Take the scenario step by step all the way to having a NY Times bestseller and you have so many definitions of "winning" it would make Charlie Sheen's head spin.

At the end of each *Let's Make a Deal,* Monty would go around the crazily-dressed audience and ask if anyone had such random objects as a wooden nickel or a bobby pin. Those who did would win some small cash amount on the spot. Not everyone who came to play ended up winning a trip to Paris, but they all had fun, and that was the name of the game.

My personal take on The Monty Hall Problem is that you do indeed start with a 1-in-3 chance of winning. But once it's down to two doors, I contend that the probability becomes 50/50, regardless of whether you change your mind or not. Genius columnist Marilyn vos Savant, however, disagrees vehemently, and has gone into exhaustive detail to explain why. Since my IQ is not in the Guinness Book of World Records and hers is, I'll graciously concede.

As for the odds of achieving commercial success as a writer, no one can predict that with any certainty. But one thing we can all agree on is that the probability of getting zonked is 100% if we don't try. Going the full Monty means writing, even when we think the odds are against us. If we love to write, and we play the game for the sheer fun of doing what we love, we are guaranteed to be a winner.

I'm just glad I don't have to dress up in a clown costume to play. Marilyn vos Savant already thinks I'm an idiot.

AS YOU MAKE YOUR WAY TO THE TOP

Over 5,000 people have attempted to scale it, and only 1/8 of them have succeeded. Mountain climbers consider Mt. Everest—the pinnacle of the earth—the ultimate goal.

Achieving our writing aspirations is like scaling a mountain. A knowledge of the craft, the proper tools, and a strong determination are essential to begin the climb. There will be obstacles on the way up and moments when you think you just can't do it. But those who make it to the top of Everest don't let difficulties keep them down. They envision the pinnacle of the mountain and focus on how magnificent the view will be from five and a half miles above sea level.

So, what is your writing goal? If you're just starting out, maybe you simply want to write a book and get it published. If you're already a published author, maybe your goal is to have a New York Times Bestseller. If you've already had bestsellers, maybe you just long for a week off to brainstorm your next story.

As I was completing this book, I had a conversation with an author who has been published regularly for years and has enjoyed success by any writer's standard. Despite her accomplishments, she harbors an innate reluctance to claim her success; to *own* it. Whether it's humility, disbelief, or a fear of jinxing a good thing, it is hard to say "I've arrived" when you feel you still have mountains to climb.

Fact is, this is a sentiment echoed by many authors. Even though they became "professionals" when they sold their first article or book, the real goal in their hearts is an ambiguous, uncharted one that they won't even realize they've reached until they get there. And when they do, they'll keep going.

A true writer writes because they love what they do. They make loyal friends along the way, supporting and mentoring other writers freely. When they achieve "success," that isn't a stopping point. They thank their lucky stars and keep reaching higher, just from the sheer love of writing. They do it for the art, not for the accolades.

When George Mallory set out to be the first to climb Mt. Everest, he was asked why. His famous answer, "Because it's there," is the same reason many of us write. It's something we feel compelled to do. It requires no explanation, nor a measurable achievement to make it a valid pursuit. It's a challenge; an adventure; a road we have no choice but to follow.

May you always find joy in your journey.

… RIGHT BRAIN WRITING

ALSO BY GARY FEARON

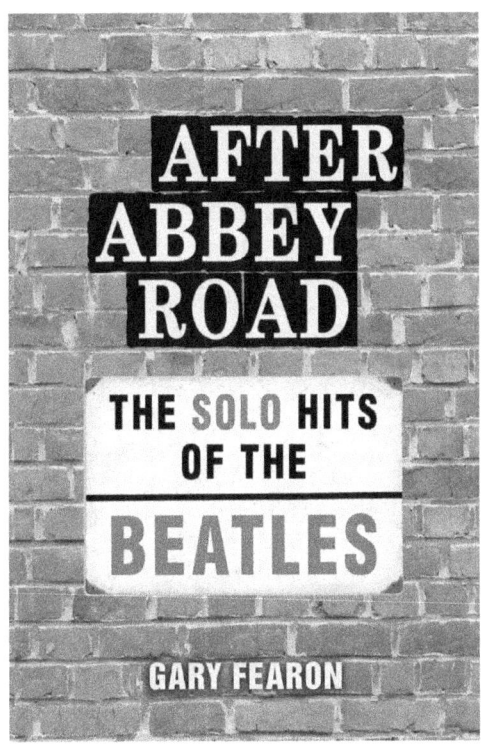

RIGHT BRAIN WRITING

www.ingramcontent.com/pod-product-compliance
Lightning Source LLC
Chambersburg PA
CBHW071958070526
44583CB00015B/1247